ART TECHNIQUES FROM PENCIL TO PAINT

TEXTURE & EFFECTS

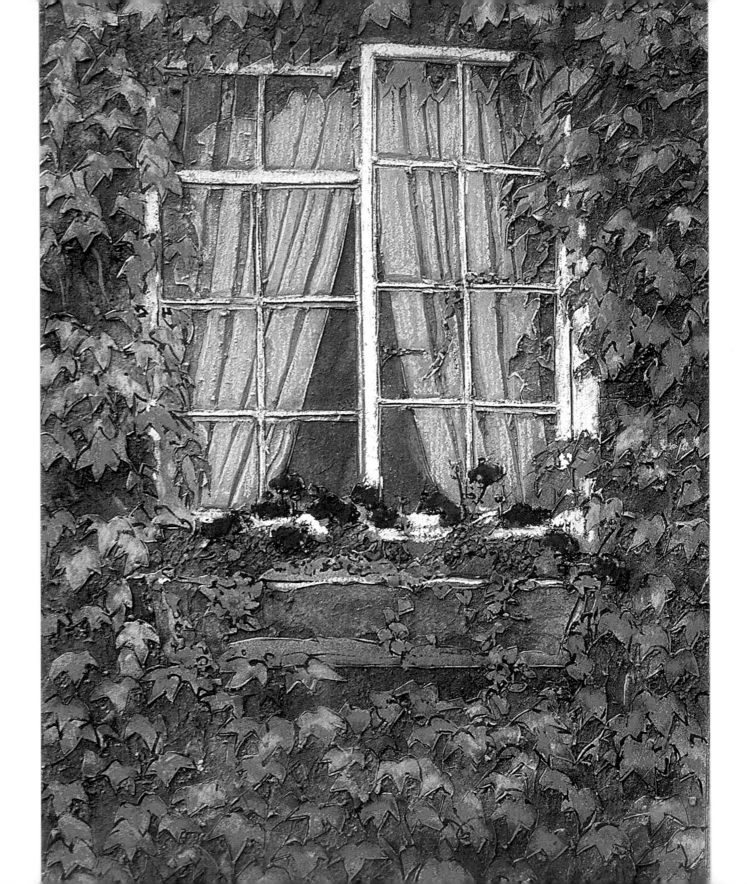

ART TECHNIQUES FROM PENCIL TO PAINT

TEXTURE & EFFECTS

PAUL TAGGART

Sterling Publishing Co., Inc.
New York

Concept, text, illustrations and photographs © Paul W. Taggart 2002

Paul Taggart has asserted his rights to be identified as the author and illustrator of this work

Series concept and structure by Eileen Tunnell

© TAJ Books Ltd 2002

Library of Congress Cataloging-in-Publication Data Available

10 9 8 7 6 5 4 3 2 1

Published in 2003 by Sterling Publishing Co., Inc.

387 Park Avenue South

New York, NY 10016

First published in Great Britain in 2002 by TAJ Books Ltd.

27 Ferndown Gardens

Cobham, Surrey, KT11 2BH

©2002 by TAJ Books Ltd.

Distributed in Canada by Sterling Publishing

C/o Canadian Manda Group

One Atlantic Avenue, Suite 105

Toronto, Ontario, M6K 3E7, Canada

Printed and bound in China

All rights reserved

Sterling ISBN 1-4027-0224-8

CONTENTS

Everyone, at some point in their lives, will be enraptured by the subtle qualities of texture. It may be moss on a wet stone, the weathered surface of a stone building, layers of paint peeling from wood, or worm encrustations on a seaside pebble. Whatever the texture, it will catch the imagination and excite the senses, so that one has to simply stand and stare.

To be able to capture and project texture in your painting is to bring it to the notice of your audience so that they too can share in your excitement.

So engaging can texture become that to many artists it develops into the mainstay of their output. There are many modern paintings that are composed of texture alone. While these could be viewed as purely decorative, it does pose the interesting question. Which is the most exciting? An organic texture created by nature or the inspiration it provides for the artist?

How much input or structure should the artist exert on the reflection of nature that he or she exploits? Can these textures be separate from nature and stem purely from the artist's imagination? Only you can decide, and it is in this exploration of the rich reservoir of possible avenues into texture that you will make your own discoveries.

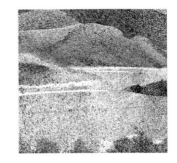

Texture can be either visual or physical. In other words, it can be real with a three-dimensional surface, or it can trick the eye with color into believing that a smooth surface is rough. It also stands to reason that some textures are both visual and physical.

The three-dimensional surface could be shallow, like a sheet of sandpaper, or deep, like the fissured surface of a rock face. If visual, the surface then appears three-dimensional, but is actually flat, or at least the depth of physical texture is only that of a layer of color.

Physical texture breaks down into two categories: arbitrary or structured. Arbitrary texture is random, or at least uncontrolled. Structured texture, on the other hand, is definitely controlled and possesses rhythm and purpose.

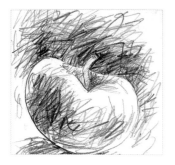

The first use of arbitrary texture was the rock faces on which prehistoric cave painters produced drawings. Part of the joy of their work is the manner in which the animals portrayed were created, exploiting the natural surface texture of the rock. While other natural arbitrary textures — such as wood grain, vegetable matter (papyrus), and animal skin (vellum and parchment) — have been used for generations, artists can also generate their own.

Any surface that has been distressed or developed has the potential to be overpainted, providing the surface will hold (or can be made to hold) the pigments. L.S. Lowry was only one of the many artists who used arbitrary texture to bring life to their work. The surface of his paintings were often preworked with stiff impasto white paint and allowed to dry for some time before he painted his subjects on them. Examine his matchstick figures and you will note that often simple strokes depicting arms and legs were rendered more exciting by the way in which they were fractured by the paint texture underneath.

I have a theory that arbitrary texture helps to bring depth to the surface because it creates a surface on which the eye has some difficulty focussing. Something that is difficult to focus on is either not there, or is only partially these in our mind's eye, hence depth.

Lowry broke his subjects up on the raised elements of the surface texture, but you can also run more fluid color into the valleys or lower section of the texture. This glazing and tonking of textures, fully explored in the later chapters, can enrich the painted surface.

Structural textures can be applied as a colorless underpainting, or may be an integral and intimate part of the paint mix. The eye tends to be caught by textures and is pulled along in the direction in which they run. By exploiting this natural tendency, the surface of the painting can begin to describe space and movement.

If the eye is moved around an object, the object appears to have form; therefore we can suggest a third dimension by this subtle use of structural texture.

This book takes you progressively through from the simplest of texture achieved with line, onto watercolor, oil and acrylic paint textures, before assuing all ideas that are intended to stimulate you into exploring other possibilities through experimentation.

You will not only discover scumbling, the most important textural technique using brushes; but also others such as spraying and stippling. Applied visual textures are incomplete without considering other tools, apart from those forming the basic painting kit. Old toothbrushes and sponges are brought into play to help you expand your idea of what constitutes an artist's tool.

Using resists is a vitally important technique within any artist's repertoire; a technique where layers of color come into play. This is an area, which by necessity, falls under the umbrella of mixed media. We take seemingly incompatible materials and use them against one another. Hence we take this natural resistance to one another to create powerful textures that are impossible to achieve in everyday use of a single medium.

Other ideas incorporate a selection of quite different approaches to both visual and physical textures. We consider the application and removal of colored layers to create soft textures, by using a medium such as soft pastel, as with soft pastel, or hard textures using a medium such as oil pastel.

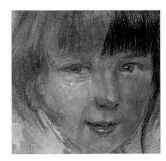

There are also exercises in scratching, wiping, erasing, tonking, tearing, cutting, distressing, and more that will allow you to achieve unusual effects and will get the creative juices going.

Finally, there is a section on compositions that exploit some of the ideas, or combinations of ideas, that have been explored throughout the book.

The process of learning about what textures and effects can be achieved is based on a willingness to experiment with materials and harnessing many so-called mistakes. Mistakes should not be viewed as failures, but rather as happenstances that can be exploited and added to one's repertoire of techniques. Many exciting results in my paintings can be described as happy accidents, and I usually take note of how they came about so that they can be used again.

This section deals with a range of everyday art materials and items that can be found around the home and shows some of the ways in which they can be exploited.

A whole host of media and materials with which you can produce textures and effects is introduced and this first section deals principally with those that are applied in a wet state.

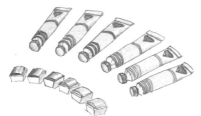

WATERCOLORS

So-called because the pigment is suspended in a water-dissolvable medium (the glue) that holds the pigment to the surface of the paper. The paint dries through evaporation. Watercolors are available in tubes and pans (blocks of color in rectangular containers). The tubes enable you to squeeze out large quantities of color onto the palette while the pans are more suited to detailed work, where only a small amount of color is required. It is always best to purchase the better quality watercolor paints, for it saves money in the long run, as the pigmentation is pure and strong. The better quality paints are also easy to redissolve when dry, thus presenting a wider scope for textures and effects.

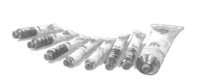

OILS

In oil paint, the pigment is suspended in an oily medium. Oils are packaged in tubes for the most part. They dry through a chemical reaction with the air, and the process is slow, enabling you to work the paint. Most manufacturers produce a range of qualities that start with the Students' Quality, which more than meet the demands that you require. As with all paints, they can be applied thin, let down with various mediums, or thick — a technique known as impasto painting. An oil painting can be produced in one session, alla prima, or in the more traditional manner of layering over time. Whereas watercolor painting is layered from light to dark, in oil painting you generally work from dark to light, thin to thick, gradually building up to the highlights.

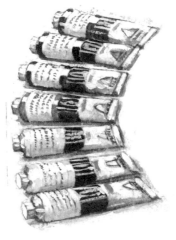

ACRYLICS

Acrylics are water-based paints in which the color is held in a "plasticised" medium. Since they dry rather quickly, acrylic paints can be worked using many of the watercolor techniques as well as in the layered style of oil painting. As with watercolors, acrylic paint dries by evaporation, which leaves the pigment sticking to the surface in an acrylic coating, thus making it impossible to redissolve. The finish can either be matt or glossy and is controlled by the nature of the medium with which it is composed.

Line Textures

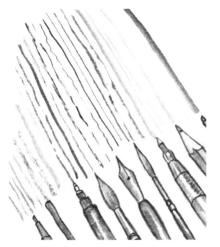

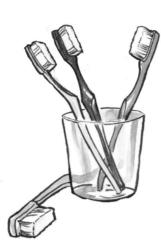

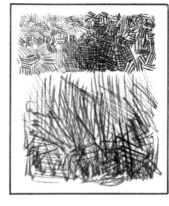

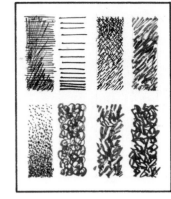

TRADITIONAL OR UNCONVENTIONAL? There are many line qualities to be mastered and a huge range of traditional drawing and painting tools available for producing them. Experimentation is the key to using the tools and discovering all of the possibilities. You will never tire of making new inroads no matter how long you paint.

It isn't necessary, however, to spend a lot of money in purchasing the widest range of tools. Look around and see what could be put to good use. Old toothbrushes for instance are ideal for producing random patterns or tightly controlled, masked-out effects.

Hatching and cross-hatching are only two of many line shading techniques. This form of line shading can be tightly controlled (top) or loosely rendered (bottom).

Try out as many tools as possible. Apply them in a variety of ways to achieve different results.

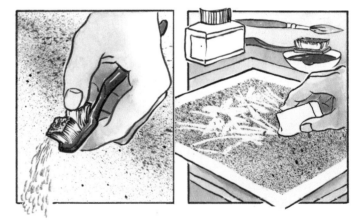

Toothbrush bristles can be used to produce a wonderful splatter effect.

An alternative to masking out. Masking fluid painted on prior to applying ink or paint with a toothbrush. Once dry, masking fluid is removed with a kneadable putty eraser.

Brush Textures

ARTSTRIPS

WATERCOLOR PAINTING

Watercolor brushes are available in a wide range of hair types, from nylon through various mixes, (depending on the manufacturer,) to pure sable, each handling in its own distinctive manner. A plethora of different head shapes are produced, with manufacturers marketing them as performing different functions.

Of all the available brushes, the round watercolor brush is the most versatile, especially in the larger sizes. For with one single brush in your tool kit, you will find that (a) fine detail is achievable with the point of the brush, while (b) large flat washes are produced using the side of the head. Ideally, a second clean, round brush is kept at hand for applying water and softening edges. A flat nylon brush is useful when color requires lifting off from an already dry surface.

When buying round brushes, look for natural pointing and spring when wet. Most stores will have a jar of water at hand to enable you to test this out.

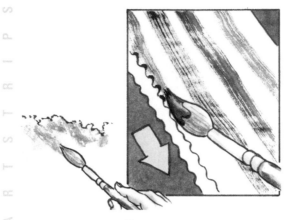

TEXTURED PURE COLORED WASHES BY SCUMBLING
Keep loaded brush "dry." Hold brush flat against surface and drag side of brush head across surface.

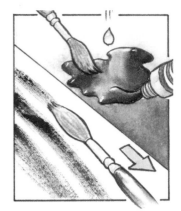

DARK COLOR SCUMBLES
Squeeze color from tube onto palette surface. Add small amount of water so color remains thick.

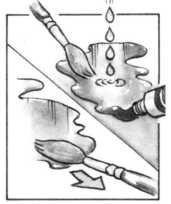

LIGHT COLOR SCUMBLES
Adding more water will lighten color. But very fluid color will flood painting surface.

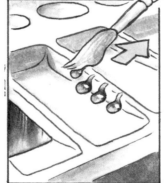

Remove excess fluid from brush head on edge of palette or carefully dab on absorbent tissue.

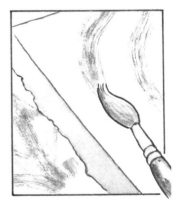

This dry brush, now loaded with light color, will scumble on surface.

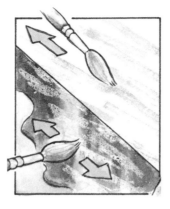

MASKING FLUID SCUMBLING
Mask out areas with scumbled masking fluid. Overpaint with color and allow to dry. Remove masking fluid using kneadable putty eraser.

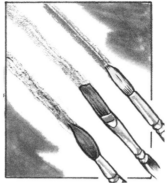

STYLES OF BRUSH
Try scumbling with different types of brush. Round sable (bottom), flat nylon (middle), oil painting bristle brush (top).

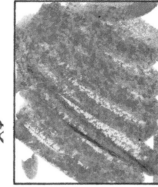

ARTISTS' DISTILLED TURPENTINE
Wet surface with this instead of water to create texture when color is subsequently applied.

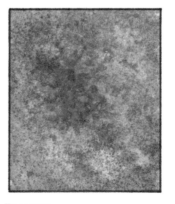

FIXATIVE
Wash over when color is still wet for a subtly different quality.

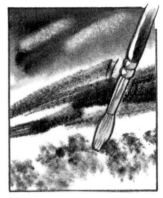

OIL PAINTING BRISTLE BRUSH
Use to scumble, stipple, and lift paint.

Brush Textures

OIL & ACRYLIC PAINTING

Any brush can be used for painting in oils and acrylics, including household paintbrushes, providing they are properly cleaned after use. However, there are brushes that are specifically designed to get the best out of both media. Understanding what they are and how they react with the paint is an essential element when working with them.

There are various choices: bristle, nylon, sable, or a mix. The filaments of each one affect the paint surface in different ways. Both nylon and sable are soft and very flexible. Nylon does, however, have more bounce, and there are new generations of nylon brushes that have been stiffened to more closely resemble bristle.

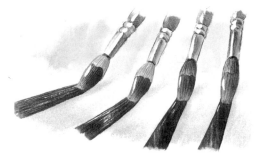

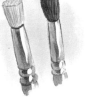

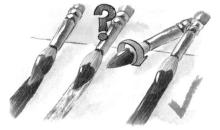

BRISTLE OR HAIR?

Bristle is stiff and as such will score through the paint as it is applied, creating a rough or furrowed surface. If the paint is also stiff, then the textures will remain in place, creating an impasto (textured) effect. This brush is most effective with stiff paint. Stiff nylon will produce a similar surface. With a softer nylon, however, this effect is reduced. This brush is best kept for glazing. Sable creates the smoothest surface.

SHAPE?
ROUND HEAD

The round head is the most traditional of all shapes, with its versatility well proven over the ages. Both the brush head and the metal ferule that joins it to the shaft are round in cross-section. A round bristle brush has a rounded blunt point, whereas the natural tapering of the sable hair produces a fine tapered point.

In use, the round bristle brush is superb at laying areas of heavy color. Its real strength lies in the fact that paint can be loaded around the whole of the circumference of the head. After a few strokes, when the paint has been depleted from one side, the brush is turned to present a fresh side on which there is ample paint to continue. This ability becomes even more important when working fresh paint onto a still-wet area of previously laid color.

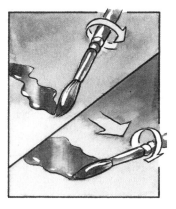

The most versatile of all the brushes is the round bristle brush. The point produces detail (top), the side blocks in masses, and for extra coverage and texture it can be rolled or rotated (bottom).

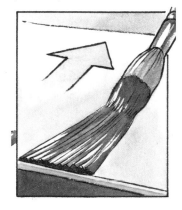

Textures are produced when raw (thick) paint is applied using a stiff bristle brush.

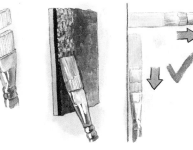
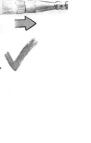

Flat

Flat in cross-section, this brush features a square tip. With only two faces to carry the paint, it naturally runs out faster than the round. The flat is, however, excellent at scumbling, presenting as it does a flat side to the painting surface. Pulling colors along, or from, edges is also made easier by its squared-off shape. The shorthaired version of the flat is known as a "Bright."

Fan

Not an essential brush for the painter's basic kit, but certainly one to have for certain occasions. The strokes produced suggest all manner of subject, such as skies, trees, and grasses, to name but a few, giving full rein to one's imagination.

Rigger

The rigger is a fine line brush, available in sable or nylon. Nylon has more bounce and thus keep its shape and lasts longer. As its name suggests, this brush is superb at creating lines that are fine enough for the rigging of sailing ships. It can also be used for any linework, including the signature on a finished masterpiece!

Filbert

This features some of the qualities of both the round and the flat brushes. In that it is a flat brush with rounded corners. This brush produces softer marks than the flat, requires frequent loading, but is sensitive to variations in pressure during application, resulting in very descriptive brushwork.

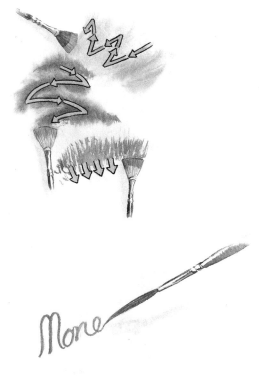

Resists

MASKING FLUID

Masking fluid is a latex solution that can be used over untouched surfaces or ink and color washes to protect all it covers from subsequently applied color. Designed to be unobtrusive when dried, this feature can render it difficult to see and thus confusing once applied. The simple solution to this is to add a few drops of Indian ink to the bottle and shake well before using.

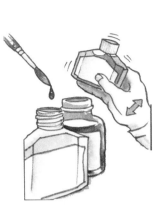

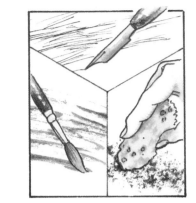

Masking fluid can be applied with a brush, pen, sponge, stick, etc. — experiment.

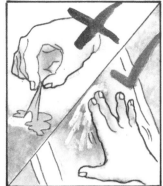

Never allow masking fluid to mix with wet paint. It coagulates and both brush and wash become clogged with rubber strands.

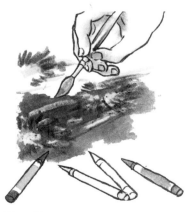

WAX CRAYONS

Ordinary wax crayons can be used to provide a textured resist.

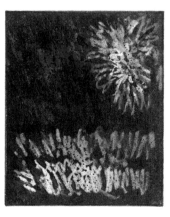

Layers of crayon can be overlaid, or under-laid with layers of watercolors.

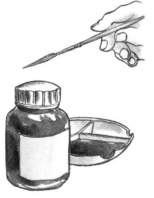

INKS

Using inks as a resist requires the waterproof and lightfast variety that contains shellac, which repels water.

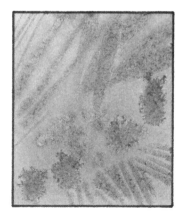

Ink resists wet watercolor washes when dropped into them. Here green ink resists a red wash.

Lift-Off

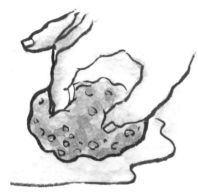

SPONGING

While there are specific artists' sponges at your disposal, there is no reason why you shouldn't start by using cheaper bathroom versions. Try different textures of sponge and different sizes to produce a range of effects.

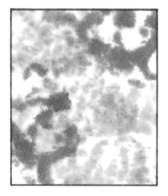

Different sized sponges and even different sides of the same sponge give different effects. Use to either dab off color or apply color.

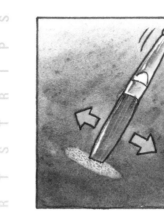
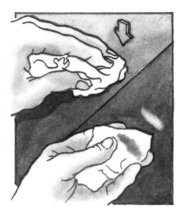

FLAT NYLON BRUSH

Ideal for lifting-off already dried watercolor. More aggressive than round sable. Brush should be slightly damp. If too wet, will leave blob of water on surface, causing uneven lifting.

Rub tip of damp brush across surface to soften and dissolve size in paper. This dislodges pigment. Immediately dab off pigment using absorbent tissue.

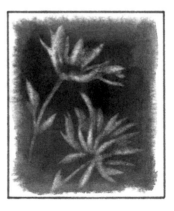
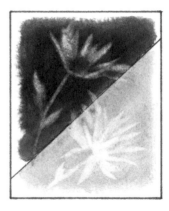

Lift-off can be used to suggest depth and volume.

This is more effective when "lifting" out of a dark value so be bold when applying wet color.

Other Ideas

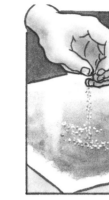

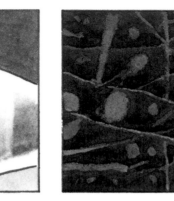

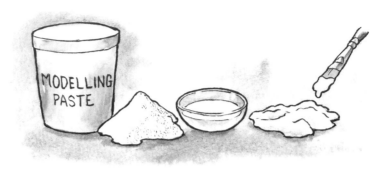

SALT
Lie board flat. Sprinkle on some salt just before paint dries. Leave to dry. Salt crystals absorb water from wet color, then dissolve, and release water again into now drying color, thus producing miniature backruns.

METHYLATED SPIRIT
Soak piece of rolled tissue in methylated spirit and apply to still-wet wash to create unusual effects.

TEXTURE/MODELLING PASTE
Acrylic texture/modelling paste can be used either for preparing a textured surface on which to paint with watercolors, oils, acrylics, and pastels or as an additive in acrylic paint mixes. Composed of fine marble dust mixed with an acrylic medium, the stiff consistency of this paste holds textures well, especially those applied with a stiff flat brush.

When used as a ground on which to paint, resultant textures provide interesting peaks and troughs for all kinds of media, from the subtlest of gentle pastel blending and oil glazes to the most rigorous acrylic strokes.

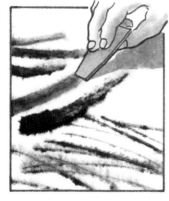

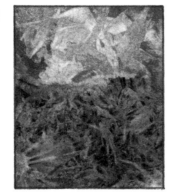

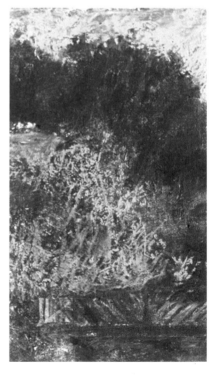

CARDBOARD
Cut spatulas from cardstock and apply tube consistency color to wet surface.

TISSUE/PLASTIC FILM
Crumple into wet wash and only remove when color has dried.

Palette/Painting Knives & Spatulas

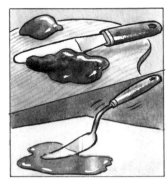

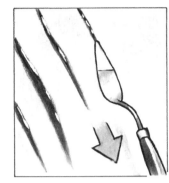

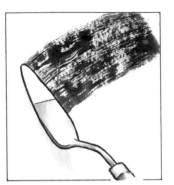

OIL OR ACRYLIC PAINTING
Stiff palette knife used for
mixing/scraping paint (top).
Flexible painting knife
(bottom)...

...for applying color.

To apply thick stroke of
color, draw loaded blade
edge across surface. Any
tube paint applied directly to
dry surface will create a dry,
scraped stroke.

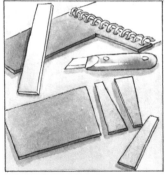

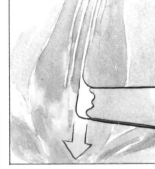

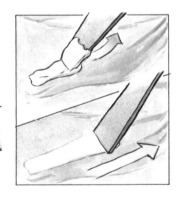

Inexpensive alternative to
painting knife. Cut spatulas
from old piece of cardstock.
Discarded backboards of
sketchbooks are excellent.

Heavily load with paint and
drag spatula edge-on to
create ridges and lines of
color.

Deposit heavy color (top).
Blend with clean spatula
(bottom).

Stretching Paper

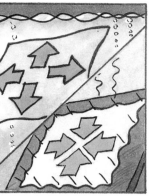
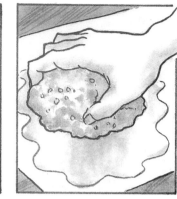
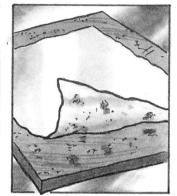

Wet paper expands. When fixed at edges, will contract and stretch as it dries.

If paper is thin, wet both sides with a natural sponge.

Wet wrong side first, as this will pick up dirt from the drawing board.

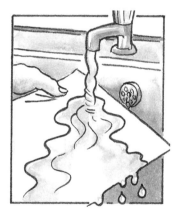
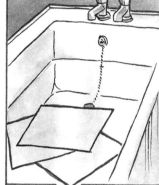
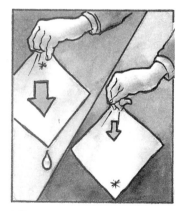

Medium to thick weight paper needs soaking through. Wet both sides under tap.

Thickest papers require thorough soaking through. Leave in a tub of cold water for at least ten minutes to ensure expansion of paper fibers.

Allow excess water to run off. Hold by one corner first, and then switch to opposite corner to ensure even run off.

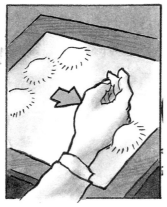

Position on drawing board and squeeze out large air bubbles. Ensure hands are clean and work out from center.

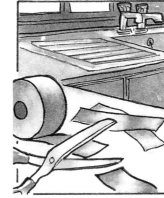

Cut gumstrip to length, allowing at least 2" (50mm) extra on each length. Keep roll away from water to prevent from sticking together into hard lump.

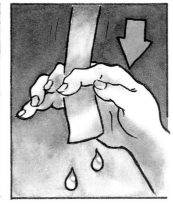

Thoroughly wet each strip by running through water in sink or bowl. Run through fingers to remove excess water.

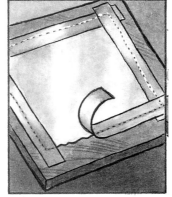

Stick paper on drawing board. Ensure gumstrip overlaps onto board. Position half width on paper and half on board.

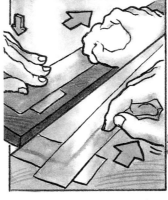

Remove excess water under gumstrip. Hold down one corner to secure. With tissue in other hand, press down and draw along length of each strip. Tissue will absorb excess water. Finally, ensure paper is securely stuck down. Run fingernail along edge of paper.

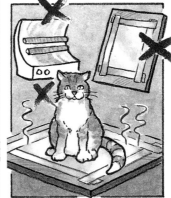

Don't use artificial heat sources to dry. Leave flat to dry naturally, but avoid unwanted guests!

Introduction

There are more ways of mixing a color than simply mixing it on your palette. The color mix can be achieved on the surface of the painting itself.

Layering transparent or semitransparent colors over one another can create mixes in depth. Spots, ticks, or small patches of color interwoven on the surface can create a visual mix, for example spots of red mixed with spots of blue will appear purple when viewed from a distance.

Putting one color next to another changes the nature of each. Complementary colors laid side-by-side, or over one another, can either make each other sing, as they respectively dazzle our eyes, or dull to a gray.

COLOR MIXING

Where the prefix letter is shown in capitals this denotes a larger quantity of that particular color.
Conversely, where the prefix letter is shown in a lower case, this denotes a smaller quantity of that particular color.
E.G.
Bp= large amount of blue-purple.
bp = small amount of blue-purple.

COLOR REFERENCE

Red-purple (Rp)
Red-orange (Ro)
Blue-purple (Bp)
Blue-green (Bg)
Yellow-orange (Yo)
Yellow-green (Yg)

Basics of Color Mixing: Primary & Secondary Colors

Three bright primary colors form the basis of the color circle and these are known as hues. These three primaries — red, blue, and yellow — mix to form secondary colors — orange, green, and purple. Mixed with the neighboring colors on the color circle, the primaries produce mixes that reflect the bias of the color with which they are combined. For example, the blue-green [Bg] with its bias toward green achieves the brightest green when mixed with yellow-green [Yg], while the blue-purple [Bp] with its bias away from green, mixed with yellow-orange (Yo), results in the dullest of greens. The value of these mixes can be lightened. In watercolor painting this is achieved through adding water. Working with an opaque medium, such as oil requires the addition of less white, which has a tendency to dull the color. Darkening a color's value is simply achieved by adding less water or white, or adding more pigment, depending on the prevailing mix.

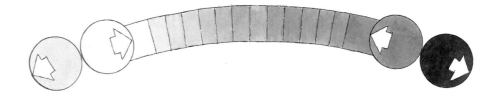

TERMS ESSENTIAL TO UNDERSTANDING COLOR MIXING
HUES
Bright primary and secondary colors are known as hues.
VALUE
Some hues are very light, while others are dark = different values.
INTENSITY/CHROMA
Dull colors have a lower intensity than the bright ones.
TONE
The degree of lightness or darkness of a neutral gray.

Surface Mixing

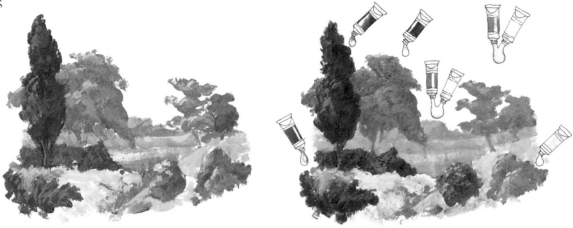

ADJUSTING COLORS IN OPAQUE MEDIUM

Adding white inevitably has the effect of dulling colors, and when combined with the use of a limited palette it can sometimes lead to a flattened color range. To return the sparkle, intensity, and range to colors, glazes and tints are employed with tremendous results. These thin layers of transparent or semitransparent color transform colors beneath them, changing color, value, intensity, texture and depth.

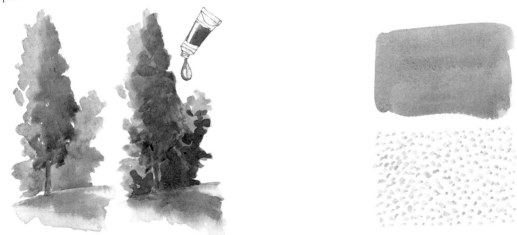

ADJUSTING COLORS IN TRANSPARENT MEDIUMS

Glazes of color can be used in watercolors to great effect. Try purple over greens for added interest in shadows. This mixing through layers is common in watercolor painting, and can be accompanied by visual color mixing where the colors remain separate as dots, dashes, or brushstrokes. The eye mixes them visually, although when you look carefully the constituent colors can still be seen. The work of the Pointillists provides an insight into the work of successful exponents of this technique.

Complemetary Colors

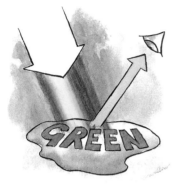
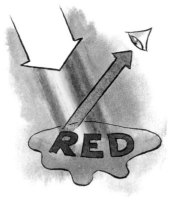
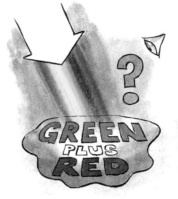
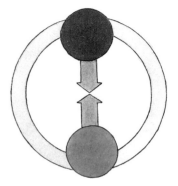

UNDERSTANDING COLOR

Pigments absorb light, and the more pigments that are in the mix, the more light they will devour. White light is a mixture of all the colors that we see in a rainbow. Take the color green for example. After alighting on green pigment all the rainbow colors, except green, are absorbed from it, thus the reflected green that is rejected reaches our eyes.

On the other hand, red absorbs all the color from white light, except red.

Thus, when green and red are mixed, the resultant mix will absorb all color from white light, in effect they are cancelling each other out. As no color is reflected, we will then see only black.

Colors that cancel each other out in this manner are known as complementary colors, and in the case of the color circle they are shown opposite each other. Hence, any two colors shown exactly opposite each other on the color circle are complementaries.

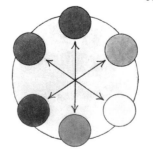
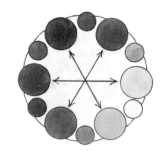

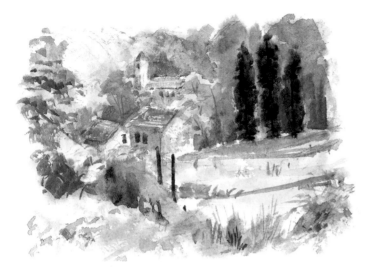

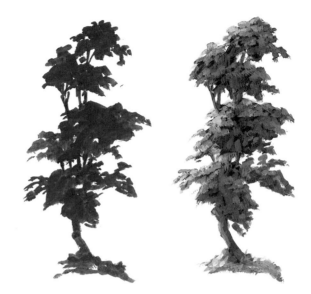

USING COMPLEMENTARY COLOR

Accents of a complementary color laid next to each other can stimulate the eye. In this exercise, the red rooves, although accounting for only a small area of the painting, are enough to excite their complementary greens, making them look richer.

Another way to excite the color is to underpaint with a complementary. This tree features thin greens, dulled to a colored gray/green mix by layering over a red underpainted layer. The tiny spots of red that are left exposed act as complementary contrasts — two techniques in one.

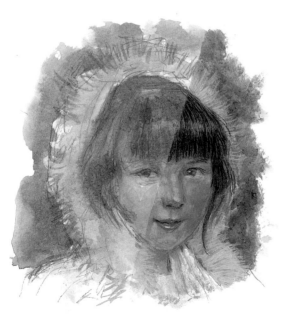

It is very common for cool colors to be used to underpaint warm, and there is a long tradition of using this idea to capture flesh tones. Green is especially useful to bring luminosity to the shadows and translucency to the skin. Note not only the way in which the green glows through the warm overpainting but also how much actual green remains throughout the rendering to kick the warm pinks and oranges into action.

Textured Color

In oil painting this method of color mixing goes hand in hand with the inherent nature in which the paint is built up in layers. You must understand this layering to know how to control color mixes.

UNDERSTANDING GLAZES

Glazing is the application of a thin, transparent layer of color in which the mix is diluted with glazing medium before it is applied. An Alkyd (resin) medium is faster drying and more flexible when dry than more traditional mediums.

A textured ground forms the basis of this example. Texture Modelling Paste was applied using random strokes of a bristle brush to a primed surface, and then allowed to dry. This exercise will let you see the depth of color in glazes and how to apply and blend them. It will also show you the way in which glazes exploit the texture and how to mix color into them. It will also show you how to darken or intensify them, without increasing the quantity of glazing medium on the surface.

Step 1   A blue-purple [Bp] glaze was applied to the left half of the rectangle, and a red-orange [Ro] glaze over the right half. A nylon round brush, was used to work the glaze into the surface in order to "discover" the texture as the glaze ran into the valleys between the raised surface of the texture.

Step 2   A clean bristle brush was then used to blend the colors into one another at the point where they meet in the center. At the top of the rectangle the brushstrokes were applied horizontally, while at the bottom they were applied vertically. Note how the brush blends more color when used horizontally. Both techniques have their place in an artist's repertoire.

Step 3   Sparing amounts of fresh color (no medium added) were then rubbed into the still-wet surface using a bristle brush, to form four oval shapes. Red-orange was used for the top oval in the red half and the bottom oval in the blue half. Blue-purple was used for the top of the blue half and bottom of the red half. Note how the color mixes, in varying degrees, depending on whether the stiff bristle can carry it down into the deepest valleys of the texture.

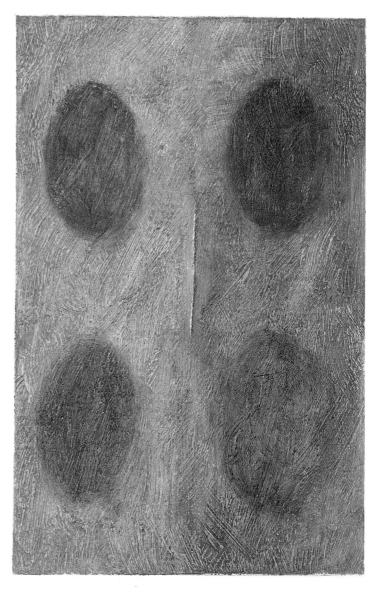

GLAZES IN USE

Further effects and textures are demonstrated in this exercise for you to follow, which is based on two separate rectangles worked up identically until the final stage. At this point both are allowed to dry and then the second rectangle is over-glazed with two different colors, to show the effect of color mixing through glazing. The exercise also serves to demonstrate the effects of removing glazes using a variety of techniques.

On a primed surface, create two rectangles identical in size. These should be created using texture modelling paste applied with random strokes of a bristle brush. Leave to dry. Work on both simultaneously, creating a pair of identical five segments as described to the right working from top to bottom. Apply a blue glaze over the entire area of the rectangles with a bristle brush to experience the difference from the exercise, on the previous page, in which a nylon brush was used. Work the glaze into the surface, exploring the available texture. The diagrams above show six sections the top is a control segment, while the five below it show the gradual removal of the glaze using a variety of techniques. This simulates the need, when painting, to remove glazes either (a) because they are wrong, or (b) to enhance the texture or vary the color mix. It is important that you continue to work with the glaze while it is still wet.

Once one of the completed rectangles has dried completely, overpaint one half with a red glaze and the other with a yellow glaze, so that you can see how all the underlying techniques affect the final mix of color and how this is intricately woven into the nature of the texture.

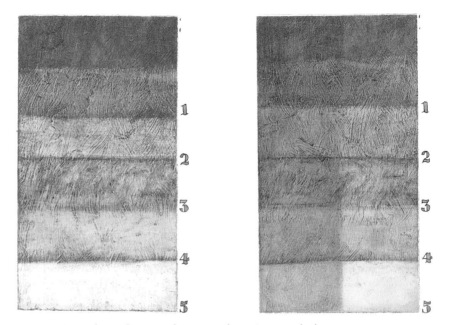

Top Segment: Since this is the control segment, leave it untouched.

Segment 1: Rub your finger across the surface to gently lift the color from the peaks of the texture, thus leaving most of the glaze on the slopes and in the valleys of the textured brushstrokes. (Suitable for small areas in your painting.)

Segment 2: Wipe the surface with a lint-free cloth. This heavier lift-off results in not only the peaks being scoured, but also the slopes of the textured brushstrokes.

Segment 3: Load a bristle brush with fresh glazing medium and work across the painted surface. The medium dilutes the glaze, making it more fluid. The medium also dilutes the glaze even further where the most friction occurs — at the peaks of the textures. The difference in density between the peaks and troughs of the texture alters the strength of the color. Excess fluid and color is lifted-off with the brush and wiped on absorbent paper towel.

Segment 4: Gently dampen a cotton cloth with Artists' Distilled Turpentine and wipe across the surface. The turpentine aggressively loosens the glaze, and the peaks of the texture will return to their unpainted state.

Segment 5: Load a bristle brush with Artists' Distilled Turpentine and work it into the surface. This dissolves all the glaze, even in the valleys. The whole solution should then be wiped from the surface with a lint-free rag. The turpentine will swiftly evaporate and leave a very matt finish. If this were a painting, you would normally brush on a layer of retouching varnish to restore the surface gloss and to protect the exposed paint layer.

29

Introduction

In painting, line is not merely something that runs along the edge of an object's silhouette. Neither is it necessarily something that is very narrow and very long. Line can be quite short and it can be found throughout the internal structure of elements within a composition.

What is important is that line should be surrounded by an area of contrasting color and/or value. It stands as an accent within its environment, a positive against a negative. Thinking of line in this manner will encourage you to become more versatile in the way you consider its application.

Line can be long and thin, but it can also be composed of dots, dashes, spirals, squiggles, circles, triangles, rectangles, hatching, and cross-hatching — the possibilities are as extensive as your imagination will allow. Resultant textures can be used separately or overlapped, or washed and drawn over with color.

Pencil drawing, both in monochrome and color, is sadly underestimated. Many people may simply have become disillusioned by what they see as a tedious medium to use. After all, who would want to build up an image of any meaningful size with only one HB pencil? If drawing is supposed to be an enjoyable pursuit, this is certainly pushing the limits. In this section we explore various ways in which pencil marks can be exploited.

If you have never used a watercolor pencil, you have yet to experience the pleasure of drawing. Dissolving the applied marks with a damp brush is almost magical and takes me back to the invisible coloring books I had as a child, where brushing clean water onto the page brought the invisible colors bursting into life.

I can more or less guarantee that at an early age you got more fun out of scribbling with a ballpoint pen than with a pencil. Why should this not be a legitimate medium in which to work now?

Did you ever have a drawing pen and a bottle of ink thrust upon you? Did it blot, scrape, scratch, or otherwise conspire to make you feel inadequate?

Then there is the brush pen. This treasure of a tool is one of my most used. While it looks like a fountain pen and features an integral ink cartridge, a flexible brush head replaces the pen point. Consequently, it affords the most fluid of lines and is highly responsive to one's every move.

This section is merely an introduction to line as texture. It is intended to start you off on your journey of exploration into an area that knows no bounds.

MATERIALS
Watercolor Sketching Pencil • Artists' Quality Colored Pencils
2B Pencil • Brush Pen with Integral Ink Cartridge
Ball Point Pen • Round Watercolor Brush
Kneadable Putty Eraser • Artists' Quality Heavy Cartridge Paper

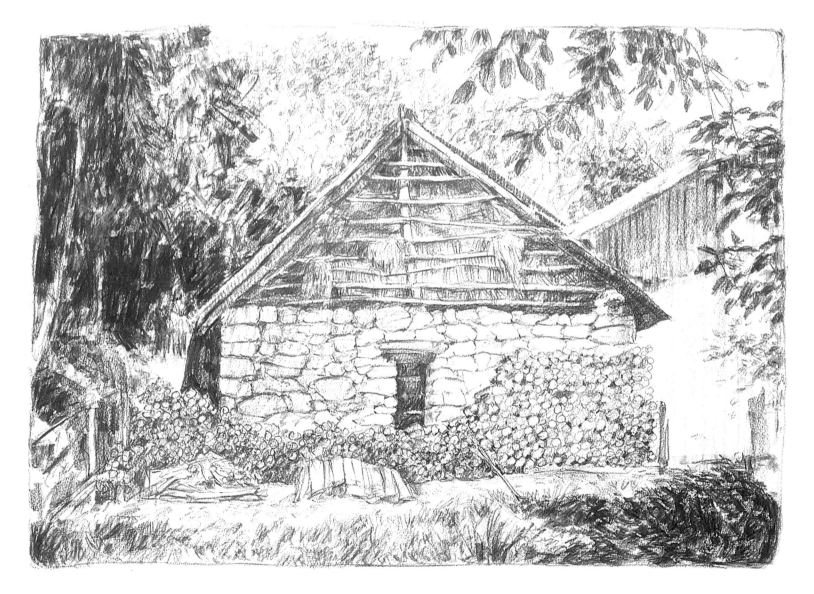

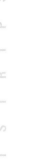

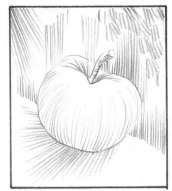

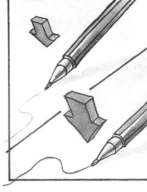

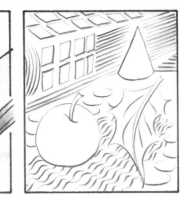

Different pressures applied to pencil yield differing line strengths.

Use creatively. Vary application to make line descriptive and suggest three-dimensional forms.

Use line for shading. This is "hatching."

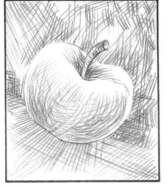

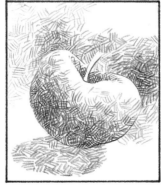

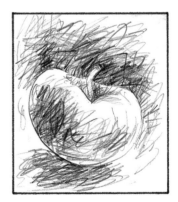

Build up layers of shading. This is "cross-hatching."

Cross-hatching can be very mechanical....

.....or fresh, loose, and scribbly.

Pencil Sketching

WATERCOLOR SKETCHING PENCIL

The graphite in this pencil is held together with gum rather than wax, thus the lines dissolve in water. Texture is developed by hatching with slowly increasing pressure, and by overlapping strokes to create cross-hatching. The softness of the pencil can vary between manufacturers, and various degrees are often available. While dry, the pencil is erasable, but once wetted and dried, the gum fixes the strokes, which consequently cannot be moved with an eraser. When wetting, create variety by not covering all of the lines. For stability, brush in the direction of the line. Use the tip of the brush for selective detail and the side of the brush head for broader wiping. Regular cleaning of the brush on a tissue prevents unwanted deposits of graphite picked up during brush strokes. Splash or spray on water for more unusual effects and irregular dissolves.

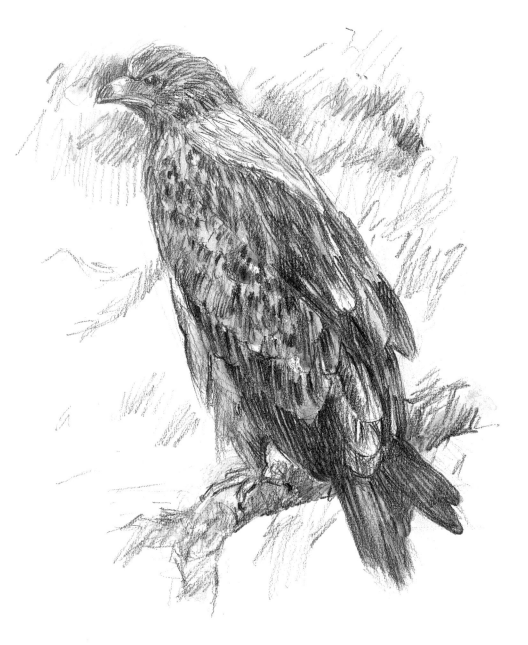

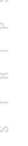

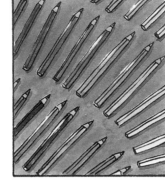

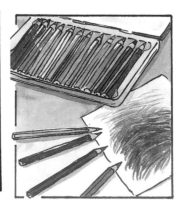

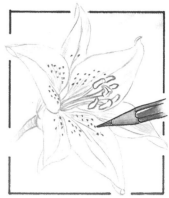

Colored pencils are a good way to begin using color. Artists' Quality are usually the most lightfast.

Artist quality available individually. Best to store in tin to keep colors in accessible order.

Now you can use colored linework.

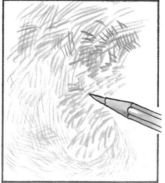

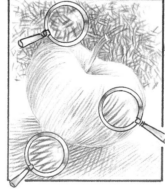

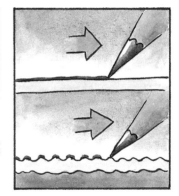

Also hatch and cross-hatch.

Layer strokes or lines of color next to, or over one another, to mix colors visually.

Paper texture will affect line quality.

Color Hatching

COLORED PENCILS

Artists' Quality colored pencils are used to capture the soft, yet structural, quality of the birds plumage. The first layer of warm yellow and cool blue is effectively used to plot the fall of light and shade across the round plump body. This is tightened up with brown hatching, a useful way to build toward complex detail — as no single line is definitive. Instead, detail slowly emerges from a soft, atmospheric thatch of lines. Final colors comprise of two values of green for the foliage and two yellow-oranges across the feather patterns. A sharp sepia line provides the final focus or accent. Since colored pencils do not dissolve in water, a felt-tip correction marker (contains thinner that dissolves pencil wax) is used to blur the focus, effectively further enhancing the softness of the feathers in parts.

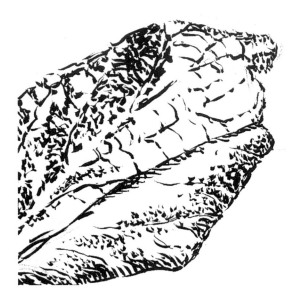

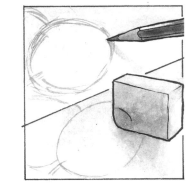

Pencil outline is essential to contain drawing. Clean away all but gentle silhouette so ink textures can be seen and controlled.

Apply ink from opposite top corner to reduce possibility of smearing slow-drying ink.

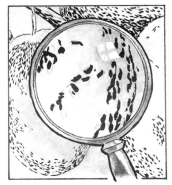

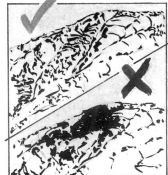

Brush pen affords opportunity to imbue dots with character, to help describe form and texture.

Overlap patterns of dots and dashes, but avoid filling in to become solid, which will flatten form and texture.

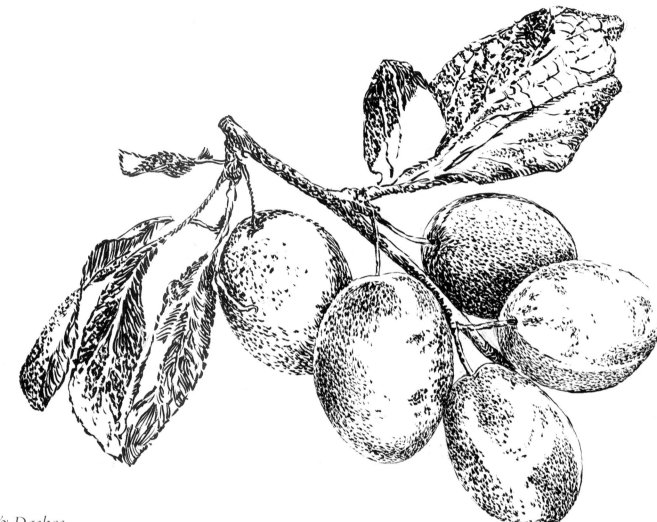

Dots & Dashes

BRUSH PEN

Start with gentle pencil outline, or the proportions are certain to go awry as you concentrate on building the texture from dots and dashes. Ensure that the pencil drawing does not become too heavy, and if it should, erase unnecessary lines. Avoid shading. If the pencil work is too heavy, you will not be able to detect the effectiveness of your ink work to come, which could include some very fine dots and dashes. Brush pen points do not deliver symmetrical or perfect dots. The hairs of the brush head leave a characteristic mark, which you should exploit as part of the texture. As you work around the shapes, leave areas or patterns of white, even at some of the edges. As always, it is often what you leave out that makes a successful piece. Look for patterns that give direction to surfaces. On completing the pen work, erase pencil lines. Before doing so, however, it is important you leave the ink work plenty of time to dry, or it will smear and ruin everything.

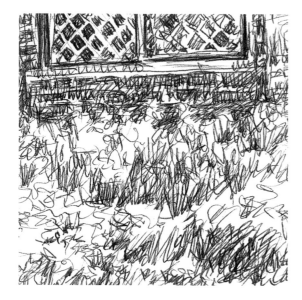

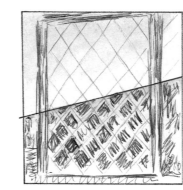

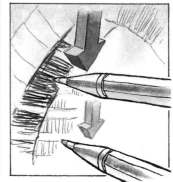

No preliminary pencil drawing. For complex areas, a simple mesh of gentle ballpoint pen lines can be reinforced later.

Achieve variety by altering pressure.

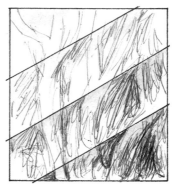

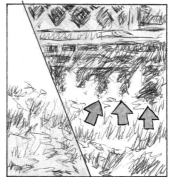

Or build up layers to really develop texture.

Start with near objects and shapes so natural overlapping and resultant negative shapes create depth.

Scribbles

BALL POINT PEN

This could be described as "taking a line for a walk." Do not bother with a preliminary pencil drawing. Simply start in the center and wander over the paper in a relaxed manner. As with all ink work, it is easier to start with the objects in the front of the picture, but there are no rules as such here. Work swiftly, so that your concentration is removed from individual strokes and is kept on the overall build up of texture. Allow your eyes to sweep across the whole drawing so that you can assess the developing contrasts. As the layers grow, real texture begins. Note how it pays to leave areas of white paper intact as a contrast and relief to the eye. Not every brick needs rendering to show that there is a wall. Our imagination pulls together the impression and suggestions to solidify the scene.

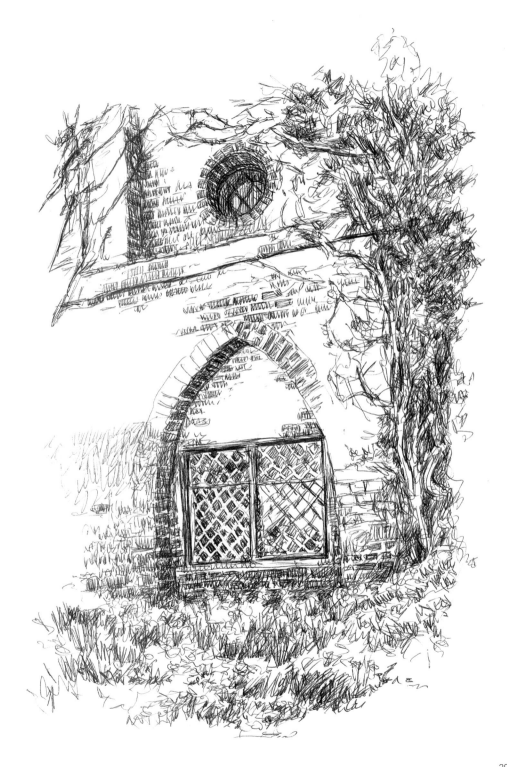

Colored Pencils

In this exercise a tin of colored pencils is used, which offers a limited palette of colors. Texture is built up, and overlaid colors mix visually on the surface to extend the limited range of available colors. Keep the hatching sharp by ensuring pencils are well pointed at all times. Defining areas with color yields more detail than using tonal values alone.

[A] Whether the area is light, medium, or dark, the paper is never completely covered. This provides the surface with an "open weave" texture.

[B] Begin with light yellow to suggest sunlight.

[C] A complex pattern such as the tiles can be drawn over a very gentle geometric grid, executed either in graphite pencil or, better still, a light blue pencil, which cannot be seen further down the line.

[D] Color mixing takes place on the surface. In this exercise blue over brown = colored gray.

[E] Brown hatching over the blue pattern of the tiles dulls these to gray.

[F] Spot colors are bright colors directly over white paper that add sparkle and focus the eye to these details.

[G] Very dark solid accents give contrast to the colors elsewhere, appearing to bring them to light. Put a finger over these accents and see how the balance of light suffers without them.

A

B

C

D

E

F

G

MATERIALS

Tin of Colored Pencils

Artists' Quality Heavy Cartridge Paper

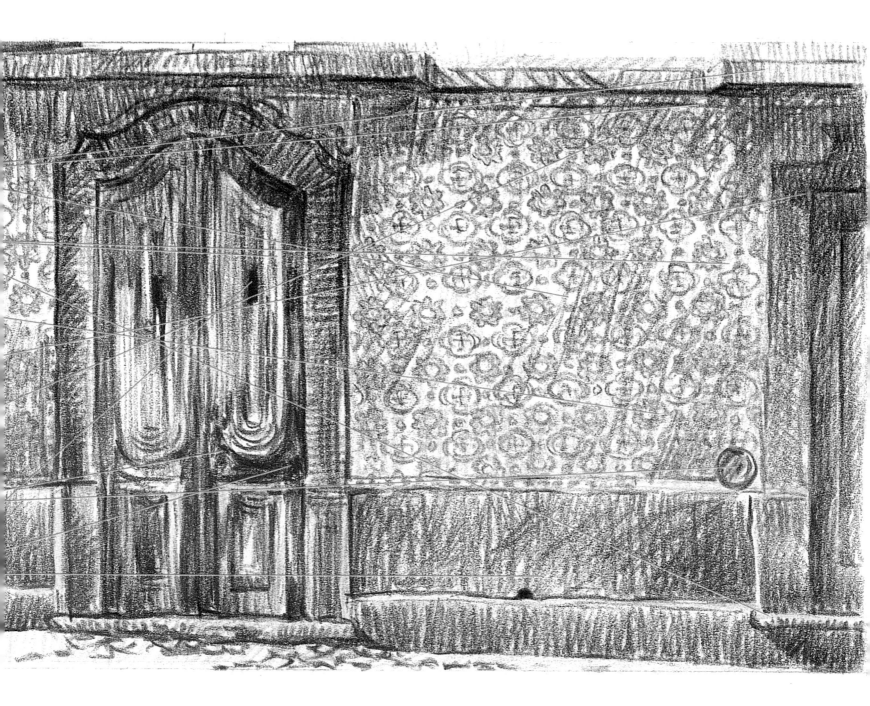

BRUSH TEXTURE

Introduction

Like many other artists, I advocate the use of big brushes rather than tiny ones, the logic of which is difficult to understand to those new to painting. Surely it is easier to manage detail with a small brush, and when a larger area needs to be filled, why not do so with several brushstrokes?

While there is nothing wrong with this in principle, there is one major problem with a small brush: it holds less paint. A size 00 brush will render a single eyelash beautifully; however, you are then faced with reloading the brush for every other eyelash surrounding each eye.

A quality large brush that comes to a fine point when wet is a much more sensible choice. Added to which the large shoulders of a bigger brush are a considerable bonus. If instead of painting with the point of the brush head you switch to using the side of the head (the shoulder), broader, bolder brushstrokes are achieved.

A large brush also offers other intrinsic characteristics that can be brought into play. When the brush becomes low on paint, it begins to drag and lay uneven color. This technique is known as scuffing, or producing a scuff and is one of the most useful textures at the disposal of an artist. Scuffing can be achieved in a variety of media: watercolors, acrylics, oils, and even pastels — where brushes aren't required.

This section concentrates purely on watercolors, to enable you to work on the control of your brush. Having mastered scuffing in watercolor, it is easy to adapt it to all other media. If you are not intending to work in watercolors or are currently working in another medium, try these exercises in the medium of your choice. You may even find scuffing in oils and pastels easier due to the stiffness and dryness of each one respectively.

The same subject has been used in all four exercises to provide an easy comparison of the differences in the available texture. Having completed the exercises, pin the results on your wall as reminders of the various textures you could exploit. In all probability you will not use all of them in the same picture. However, until you get used to them all, it is easy to lose sight and forget about them.

Three of the four exercises, spraying, stippling, and sponging color, are common to all wet media. "Knifing-out" is particular to watercolor, but in oils you can scrape off, as the color takes so long to dry.

MATERIALS

Rough Watercolor Paper

Watercolor Paints

No. 12 Nylon Round Watercolor Brush

No. 12 Nylon/Sable Round Watercolor Brush

Nylon Flat Watercolor Brush

Nylon Rigger Brush

Bristle Brush

Waterproof Drawing Ink

Aquapasto Thickening Medium

Watercolor Texture Medium

Masking Fluid

Kneadable Putty Eraser

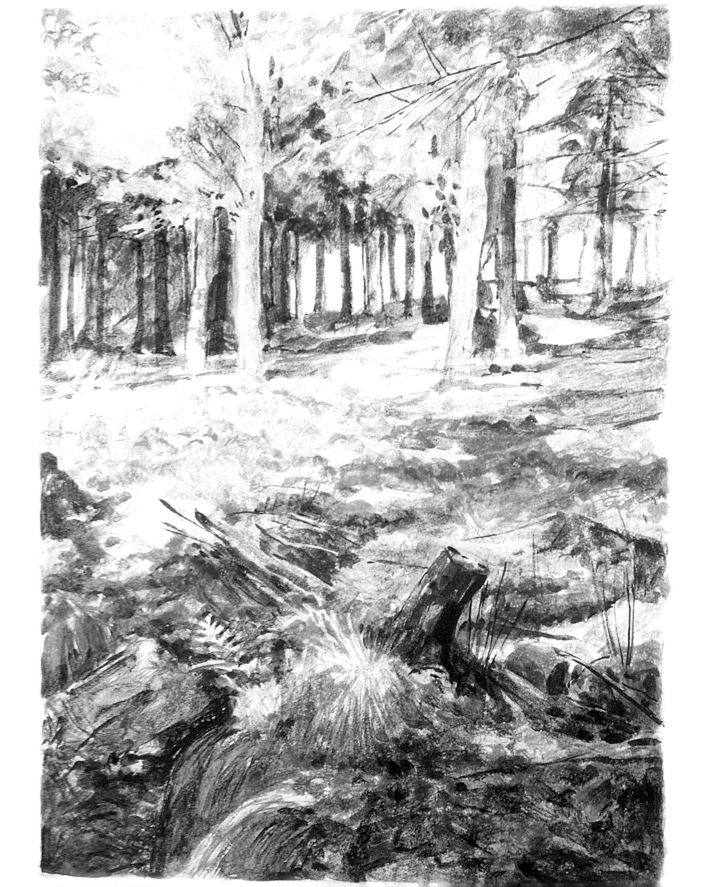

Scuffling & Scumbling
MONOTONE

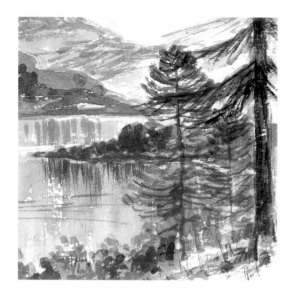

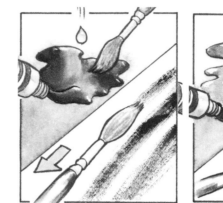

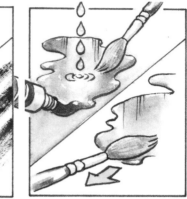

Keep brush dry by (a) adding small amount of water to color squeezed from tube. This thick mix scuffs easily and gives dark color.

(b) Adding more water lightens color, but fluid mix will flood painting surface....

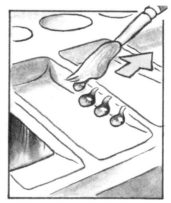

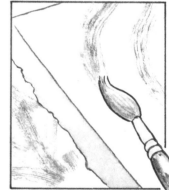

...so remove any excess fluid from brush on edge of palette or on absorbent tissue.

Thus light, dry brush mark is easily scuffed on to surface. Test scuff on spare paper before applying to painting.

SCUFF or SCUFFS
Single textured stroke or group of single texture strokes
SCUMBLING
Multiple strokes overlapping to make up an area of even/regular texture

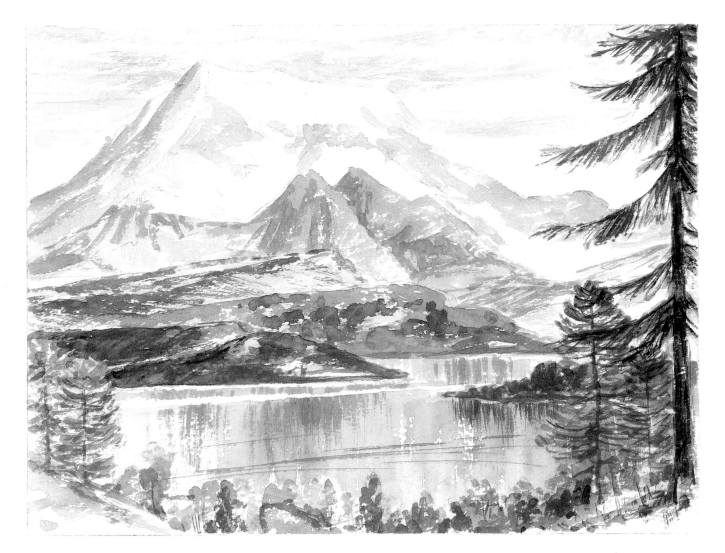

Stretch a sheet of textured watercolor paper (rough) and scuff with increasingly dense washes of black watercolor, using the No. 12 nylon round watercolor brush. Keep the brush dry to increase texture. Once the first layer is applied, the color becomes easier to apply, as the dried gum on the surface is receptive to the second coat. Round brushes easily follow the contours of sky and mountain, but the vertical strokes for the water are more easily laid with a nylon flat "wash" brush. Work progressively from the back, increasing the pigment in the mix so that you should achieve mid tones by the time you get to the foreground. Apply a second layer of scumbling from the lower mountains down, working with increasingly thickening paint mix so that by the time the foreground tree is reached the color can be almost undiluted.

Scuffling & Scumbling
COLOR

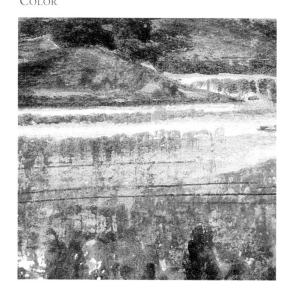

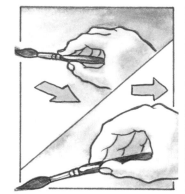

Try holding brush overhand to present greater surface area of brush to paper.

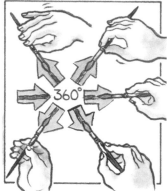

This allows more freedom of movement and brush can be drawn in direction of required brushmark.

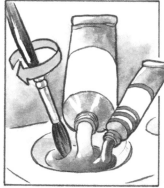

Aquapasto, a thick painting medium, is useful for mixing with paint to create buttery consistency.

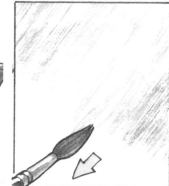

This makes dry scumbling with light tones of color much easier.

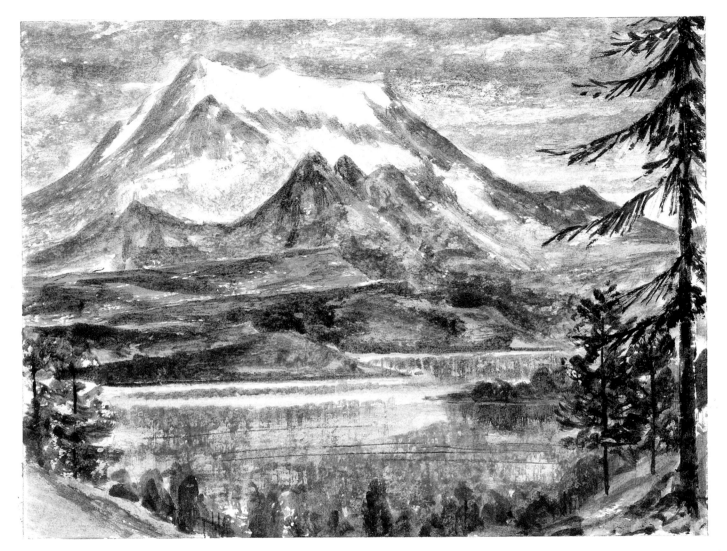

An alternative to aquapasto, watercolor texture medium contains fine particles of sand or silica and is a translucent medium that has little effect on the color, but does increase texture. In this exercise it is used throughout the watercolor scuffs, but becomes very dominant when layers of color are overlapped. Whether the second layer contains the medium or not, the first layer accepts the wet color irregularly. This medium increases the scuffing effect, but results in a more diffuse texture than you would expect from a normal scuff rendered without it. Layers of color can still be lifted, even after drying in the usual fashion. However, the presence of the fine particles makes the lift more erratic. While this can be frustrating, it does, however, offer another unique texture. Before trying this technique in a more serious composition, test it out on a spare piece of paper to discover the amount of paint lift that occurs under differing degrees of wetting. Carefully observe where colors of the same family have been over-scuffed against those that are opposites on the color circle.

47

Masking & Spraying

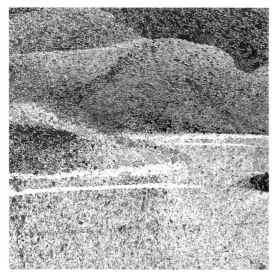

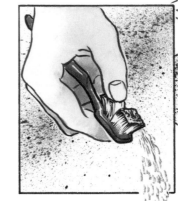

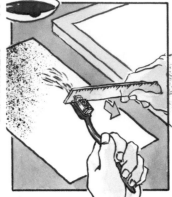

Old toothbrush bristles are excellent for creating spatter effect.

Always test strength of spray before applying to your work.

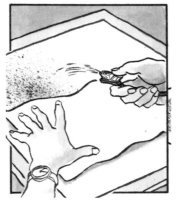

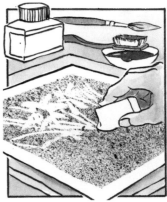

Cut out paper shape to act as mask to protect splattered areas.

Masking fluid also useful to protect irregular areas from splatters. Remove with kneadable putty eraser.

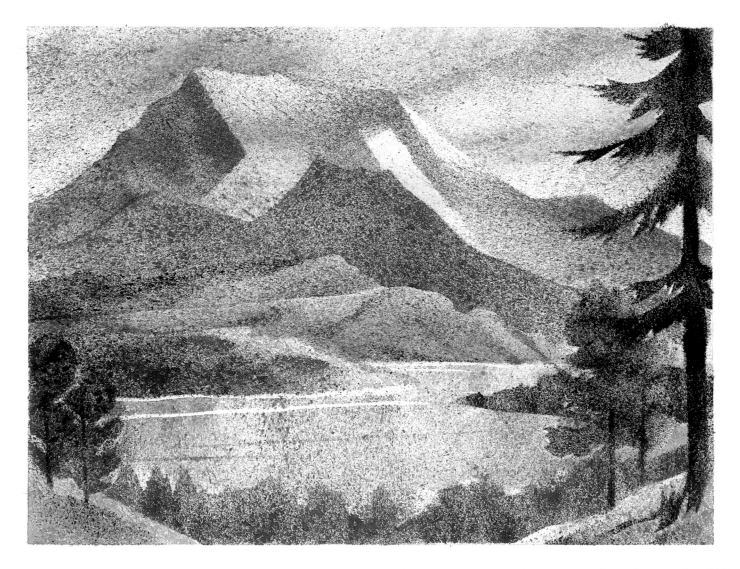

While paper masks are feasible, you may wish to use the same masks for this exercise and the next. A sheet of transparent acetate is ideal for this. The mountain, lake, and foreground are all cut from one piece, but the trees on either side require separate masks. Sketch out the composition on your surface, lay on the acetate, and mark out the mask outline using a waterproof felt tip pen. Remove and place the acetate on a cutting board. Working from the top of the picture, carefully cut out each area using a sharp knife. Place back over the surface and spray with mixes of watercolor. Different angles and levels of spray result in a variety of textures. The trunks on the smaller foreground trees were sprayed into the gap between two sheets of paper laid next to each other.

Stippling, Sponging & Knifing Out

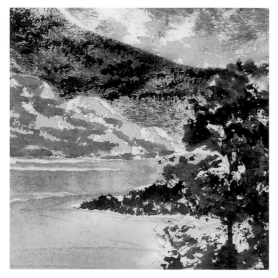

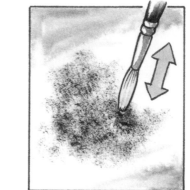

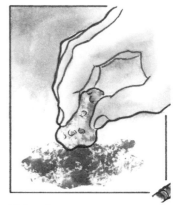

STIPPLING. Use stiff brush, such as oil painter's bristle brush to stipple paint. Try with and without aquapasto.

SPONGING. Artists' sponges yield wonderful natural textures. Each slightly different.

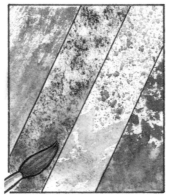

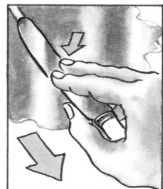

To "lose" these textures, simply apply damp brush before they dry.

KNIFING OUT. Hold blunt kitchen knife nearly flat to surface. Press blade into wash and pull. Be careful not to cut or tear surface.

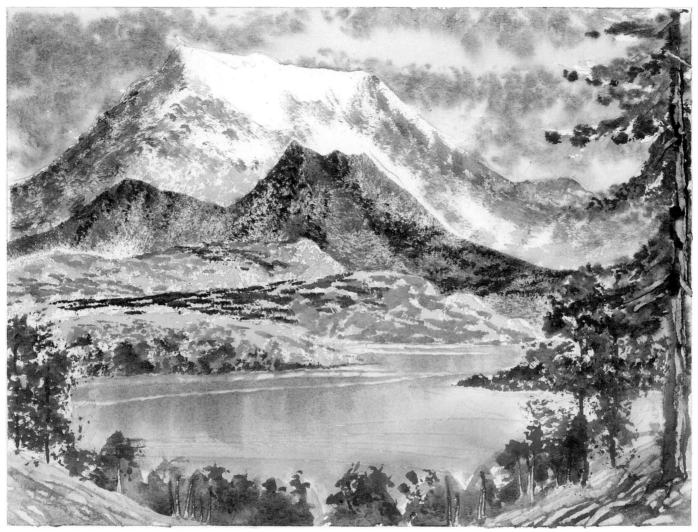

Use the same transparent acetate masks prepared for the previous exercise. Apply watercolor washes to the foreground, including the trees and water, and then knife out in different directions. The ground is knifed out haphazardly, while on the tree trunks the knife is drawn upward. Note how this is most successful in the distant water. In this exercise the strokes applied for the water in the foreground, filled in (through having been completed too soon). The paper, being damaged, then became darker with the inflowing color. Be bold with the knifing out; make definite marks with no hesitation Even if they go a little wrong, the confidence with which this has been carried out will get you through. A sponge was used here to apply the color for the waterside trees and the small green trees either side. The large tree on the right and the sky were applied in the same way. Note for yourself, whether these sponged marks are sharp or soft (i.e. wet-on-dry or wet-on-wet). Stipple the hills in a variety of colors. Note particularly the contrast along the edges or silhouettes of the hills and mountains (i.e. counterchange — dark against light, light against dark).

Scuffs, Scumbles & Masking Fluid

Scumbles and masking fluid give texture to the stonework of this disused
Portuguese gateway and the grasses that surround it.

[A] Scuffed masking fluid creates textured highlights when removed.
[B] Ink line dominant in even the darkest areas.
[C] Layered scumbles from light yellow, through orange, to brown.
[D] Warm yellow and orange scuffs provide the warmth of sunlight.
[E] Cool blue-greens suggest the contrast of shadow.
[F] Alternate light and dark areas create volume as well as texture in the
     undergrowth.
[G] Counterchange (light against dark, dark against light) provides the maximum
     contrast available to create light.
[H] Irregular perspective lines carry our eye down the path and into the distance.
[J] Static horizontals and verticals arrest eyes and provide an area of calm.

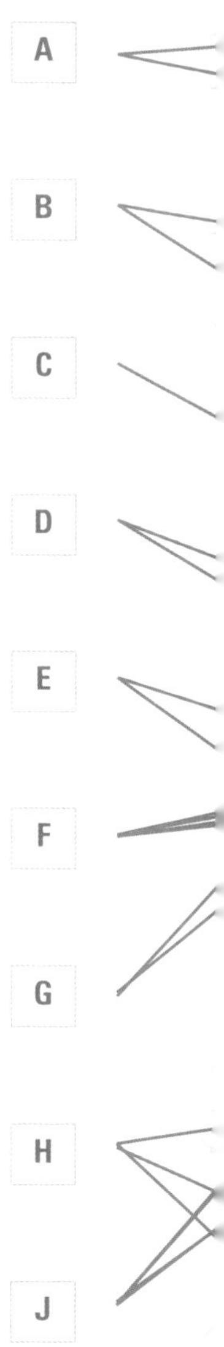

MATERIALS
Rigger Brush
Round Brush
Ink
Watercolor Paints
Watercolor Paper

A

B

C

D

E

F

G

H

J

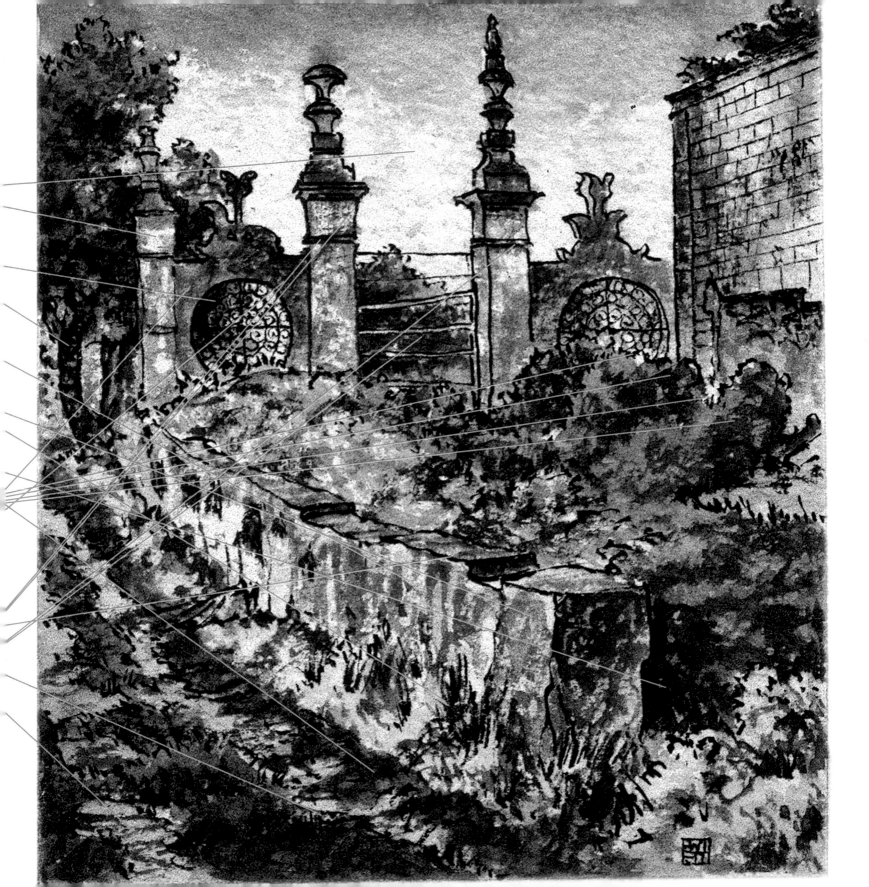

Introduction

Using resists to create texture is one of the most exciting, yet challenging, methods in the artist's repertoire. The textures they produce are powerful, and the results can be a surprise, even to the most experienced hand. If the surprise turns into shock, you must either be prepared to live with it or have some method by which the result can be modified. Generally, the more resists are applied with gusto, the more delicious the result. Allowing things to happen in painting is what keeps you on your toes and always ready to start the next piece.

The use of masking fluid is probably the most controllable of the techniques in the following exercises, since once applied, it can be easily removed from the surface. The resultant effects may be softened with lift off (in the soluble medium of watercolor) or painted over, either transparently - as in ink and watercolor - or opaquely - as in acrylics.

With more permanent resists, such as wax or wax crayon, the effects are less easy to disguise or remove. However, it is still possible to apply more color over wax by brushing with greater vigour. Having stronger adhesion, acrylic paint can usually be made to cover wax, although it is important to avoid the results from appearing too heavy.

Inevitably, some painters like resists and use them wherever possible, while others will only occasionally employ the techniques. Many professional artists are totally opposed to the use of resists, particularly masking fluid, for, they feel it is akin to cheating.

I, on the other hand, find masking fluid absolutely indispensable. Imagine trying to paint around a spider's web for example. The difficulty in painting such delicate lines can be relieved considerably by masking out the spidery patterns.

The clue to getting enjoyment out of painting is to ignore other people's preconceptions of what constitutes good painting practice or, for that matter, what you, as an individual, should or should not do.

There are those who are nervous about working with masking fluid, because they believe it can damage brushes. Early experiences of masking fluid drying on a brush are usually the root of this fear. The natural reaction to this is to use old and deteriorating brushes. Since masked areas are either highlights or points of hard-edged focus, to render them with one's worst brushes seems somewhat counter-productive!

On occasions I use my most expensive sables when working with masking fluid; the trick is simply to keep the latex mask from drying in the brush head and hairs. I do this by working a little bit of soap into the fibers. By doing so a barrier is created to reduce the penetration of the latex through into the hairs. My brush is constantly cleaned, and should any masking fluid dry, it is gently removed with an oil painting thinner, such as Artists' Distilled Turpentine or Odorless Thinner. Once washed thoroughly in cool water, soap is again worked into the hairs to remove any remaining thinner and to restore the barrier.

NOTE: While watercolor is used throughout this section to demonstrate the techniques, the exercises can also be carried out in inks and acrylics.

MATERIALS

Watercolor Paper • Watercolor Paints •Nylon Round Watercolor Brush • Nylon Rigger Brush

2B Pencil • Wax Crayons • Waterproof Drawing Ink • Masking Fluid

Kneadable Putty Eraser

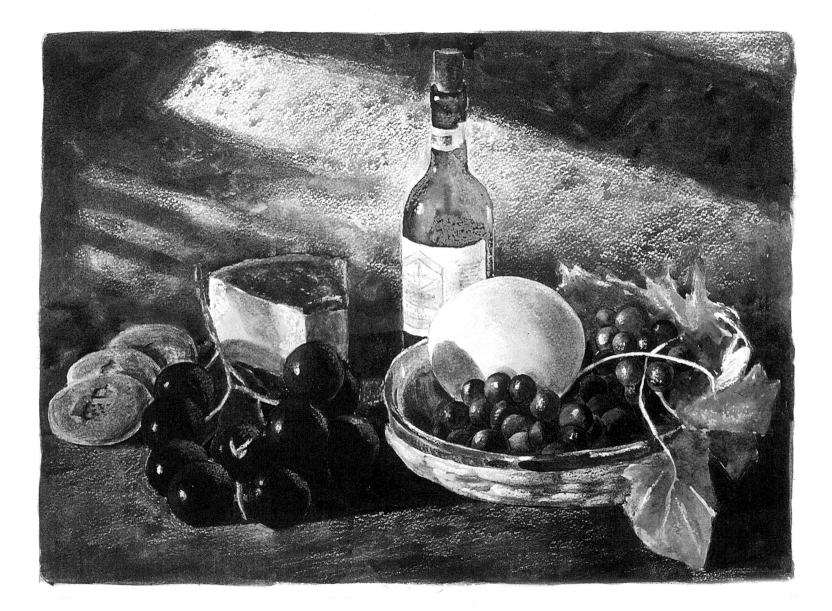

Hot Wax Resists

Using hot wax as a resist to watercolor is a technique not unlike that of Batik. For this exercise I melted down a large chunk of white candle wax. For safety reasons, this must be done very slowly on a low heat with the candle placed in a flame resistant container on a solid hot plate. Do not under any circumstances do this on an open flame or within any distance of a naked flame, as wax is highly flammable. Keep the wax warm to maintain its fluid state, but beware of allowing it to become too hot. If bubbles appear around the hairs when the brush is dipped into the wax it indicates the wax is too hot and should be removed off the hot spot until it has cooled down slightly. To clean brushes, use warm water and soap while the wax is still soft. Use cheaper/older brushes for this.

Lightly sketch out the composition using a 2B pencil. Apply the first layer of light color, blocking in main highlight masses. The use of wax resists will force you to be bold with your brush strokes, as the resist itself is quite dramatic. Allow the painting to dry before moving on to the first layer of wax resists, applied with a round nylon watercolor brush. These wax resists are used to permanently protect either areas of unpainted white paper, or areas of specific highlight colors. Move on to the second layer of color, concentrating on the medium values before applying the second layer of wax resists. Finally, finish off with dark accent colors.

NOTE: This technique can also be used for working with thin layers of acrylic paint and gouache.

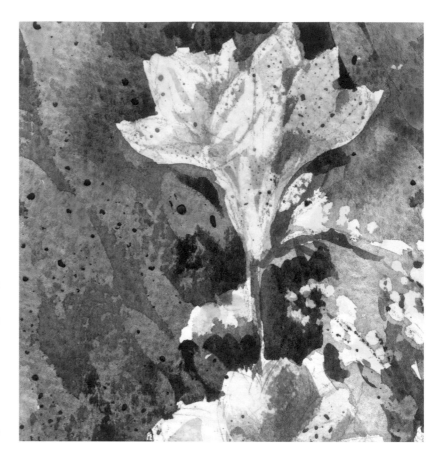

TIP
Since the function of the layer of wax resist is to protect underlying colors from being overpainted, it is important that the wax itself does not blot out the color. Because the wax dries swiftly during application, over thick areas may have a tendency to develop a white bloom, thus blanking out the underlying color. To rectify this, simply blast the area with warm air from a hair dryer, which will melt the wax into the paper, allowing the colors to show through.

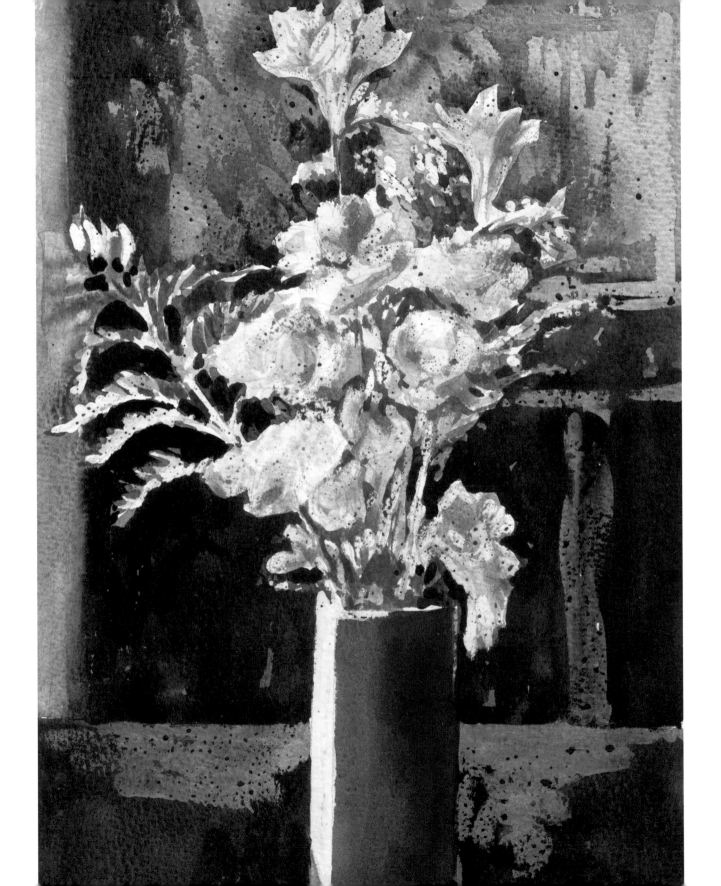

Cold Wax Resists

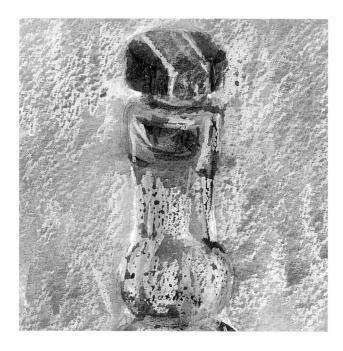

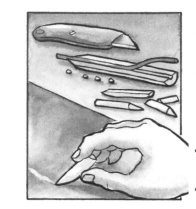 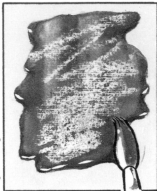

Use either white crayon or a candle for cold wax resists. Chop candle into sticks, removing wick. Vary pressure to apply different amounts of wax.

Wax resists overlaid color and echoes texture of paper.

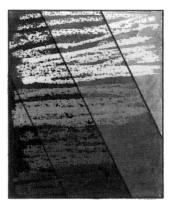 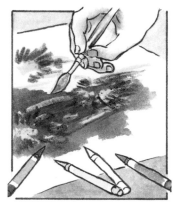

Wax resists can be used at any stage of painting. Being transparent, its will show through as underlying color.

Wax crayons give similar textured resist, but applied wax marks are colored.

Work on a reasonably large scale; this will encourage you to be dramatic and gestural with the strokes of applied wax resist. Unlike the hot wax technique, the white of the candle wax in this technique will show to some degree, just as colored crayons will, consequently altering the underlying color to an extent. Test this out by laying a wash of blue watercolor on a scrap piece of rough watercolor paper. Draw over this using a yellow wax crayon. The crayon marks become yellow-green, where the blue from beneath shines through. Now wash over this in red watercolor. The initial blue wash will become purple, whereas the wax resists the wet color, so that the previously applied wax strokes remain yellow-green against the purple.

This exercise is created in three layers of watercolor wash, with wax crayon resists applied before each one. Imagine the permutations this affords you! There are exciting, dramatic textures inherent in this technique. Throw yourself into this one and simply let things happen naturally.

NOTE: Aim for warm colors over cool and vice versa. Allow watercolors washes to change in color and strength as they move across the surface. Both qualities will enliven the contrast between washes and the textured crayon strokes.

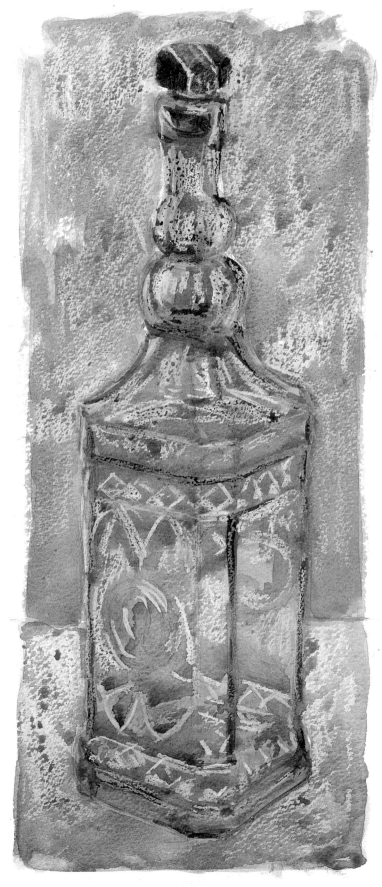

Ink Resists

A purified varnish known as shellac carries the pigment in waterproof inks, whereas in watercolor it is Gum Arabic that fixes the pigment to the surface. When the two meet in a wet state, the difference in surface tension causes a reaction, with the watercolor repelled by the ink. On drying, the shiny ink features a richer depth of color than the slightly flatter watercolor. These differences can be exploited to good effect, placing this technique in the category of mixed media.

To produce this exercise you must work on a flat surface, as the applied watercolor must be kept wet until the ink is added. The ink forces the pigment to the edges of the color washes, effectively reinforcing the silhouette. While the paper texture is enhanced, applying more than one layer of this mixed technique will begin to make the painting look dirty. Try a variation to this: drop clean water into watercolor areas and vice versa.

Notice how the yellow ink glows against the slightly duller green and purple watercolor. Watercolor always loses some of its intensity on drying, while the ink retains its gloss and depth.

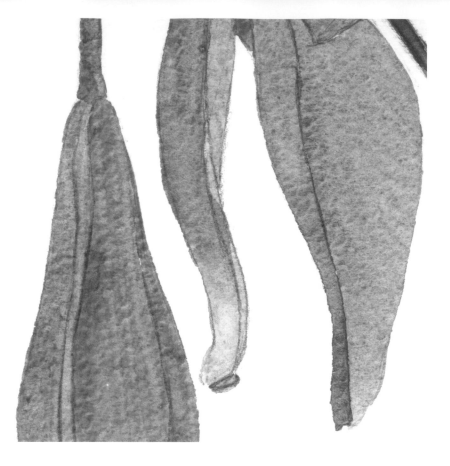

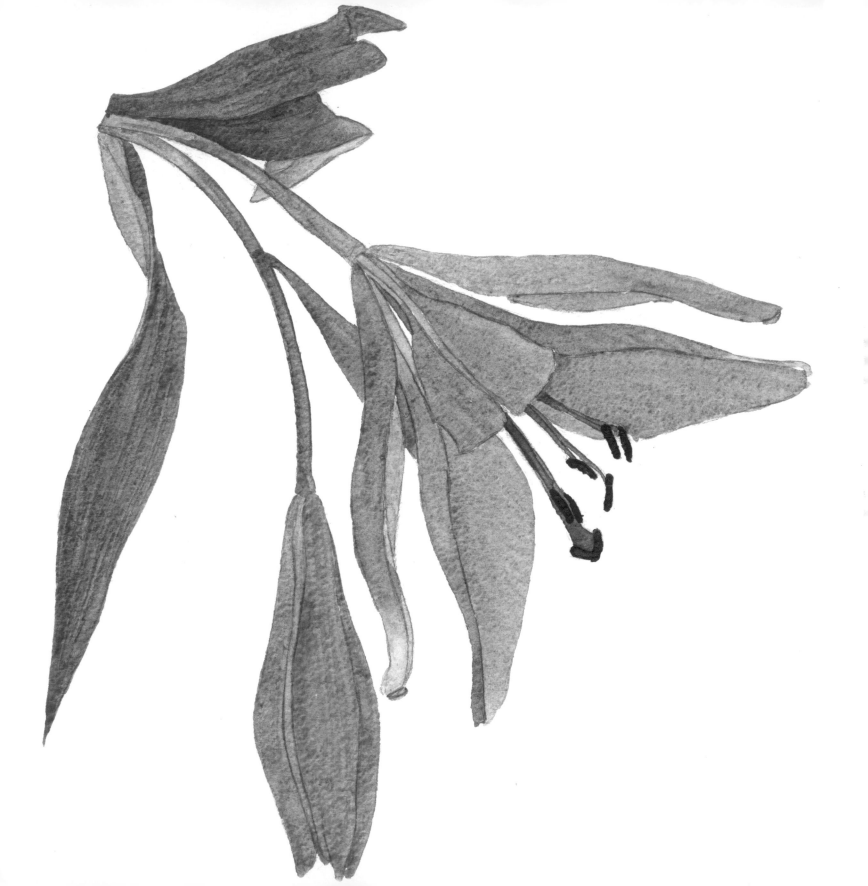

Masking Fluid

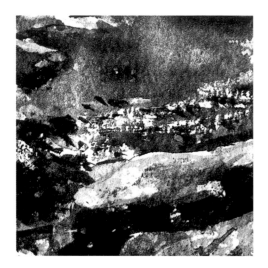

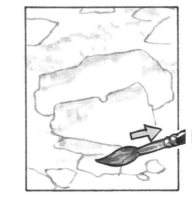

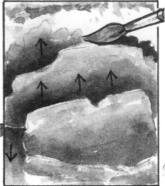

PAINTING ROCKS
Gently sketch in a group of rocks. Scumble masking fluid along top of rock edges to protect highlights. Selectively scumble mask between large rocks to suggest light catching smaller stones.

Loosely block in shadows. Place darker color behind top lit (masked) edges to increase contrast known as "negative painting."

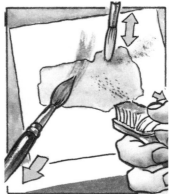

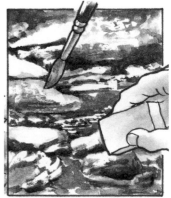

Once dry, apply textures by scumbling, stippling, or splashing color. Use paper mask on some areas.

Remove masking fluid with kneadable putty eraser and selectively drop color into exposed white areas.

Rocks make a wonderful subject on which to practice wet-on-dry painting. In order not to overwork the study, try not to use more than three layers of color in any area. This way, you will ensure the transparency of the color, even when at its darkest. The first washes establish the light colors — note how these are warm yellows and green toward the center of the image, moving toward cool blues and green as they radiate out toward the outer edge of the rectangle. Color is used to focus our eyes centrally within the picture. When dry, protect highlights using masking fluid. Ensure these are applied as loosely as the color, scuffing and scumbling to create shimmering highlights. The second layer of color is used to establish the darks in the rich shadows. Note the rhythms and directions within these darker areas and where they have hard or soft (lost) edges. Cool colors are laid over warm and vice versa, creating subtle surface mixes of infinite variety — impossible to attain in a palette mix. Once this layer has dried, remove masking fluid with the kneadable putty eraser and scumble on bright colors into the highlights. This softens their silhouettes while retaining their clarity.

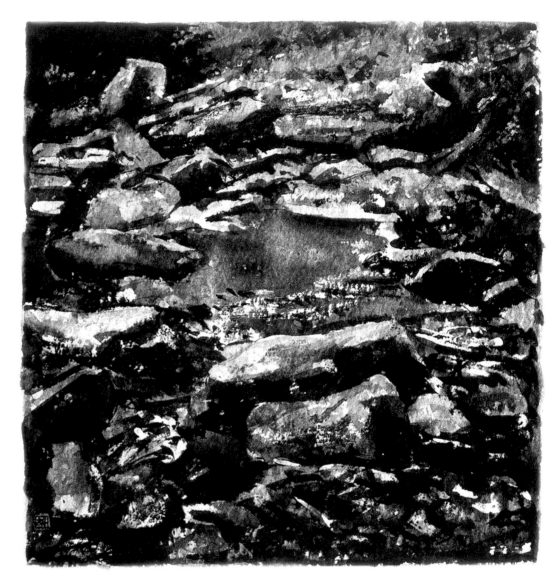

Cold Wax Resists

Color washes in this exercise have been separated by applying layers of wax resist, creating a textured surface across the face of this highly distressed door's surface.

[A] Waterproof ink linework that is strong enough to be visible through the darkest overlaid watercolor washes.

[B] Rigger brush responds to differences of pressure to give a variety of line thickness from the same brush.

[C] Gently draw rigger brush swiftly across surface to produce scuffed line that perfectly matches the distressed nature of the door.

[D] First two cold candle wax resists protect the white of the paper to produce bright highlights.

[E] Cool colors laid over warm, thus the resists create a surface mix of colored gray texture.

[F] Several layers of rich color can be applied to the dark areas. These shadows are full of color — never use black or gray.

[G] Areas involving several layers of candle wax and color are impossible to rigorously control. The wax is difficult to see before the color is applied, therefore the results can be surprising. Washes applied with deliberation and extra pressure may provide a little more coverage, but generally go with the flow and allow the resists to develop.

A

B

C

D

E

F

G

MATERIALS
Rigger Brush
Round Brush
Waterproof Drawing Ink
Watercolor Paints
Watercolor Paper
White Candle

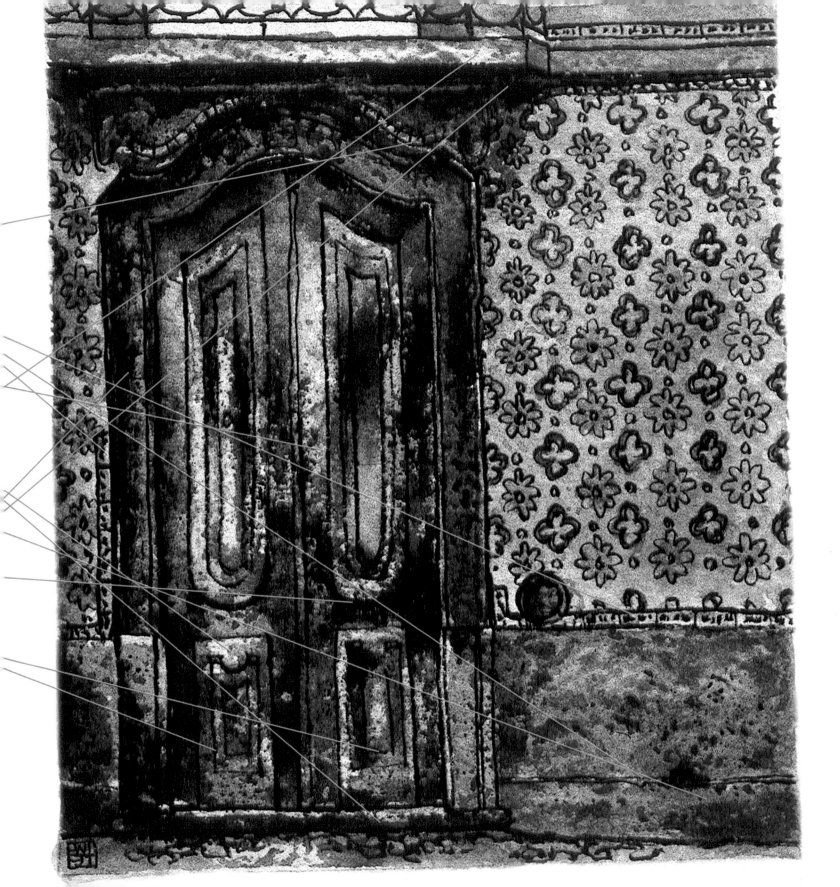

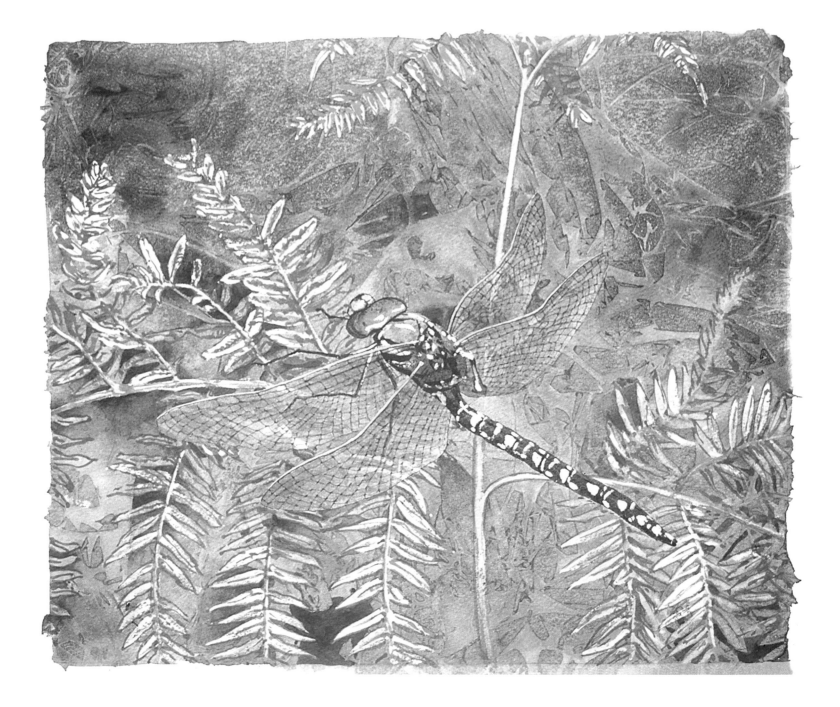

Introduction

Ordinarily, one would associate the removal of surface material as being a correction. This however is only half the story.

In pencil drawing such action need not only be utilized for eradicating a mistake. Full or partial erasure of the graphite is an invaluable technique in its own right.

As we move into watercolor, it is possible to remove applied dry pigment from the surface, thus exploiting the medium to its fullest. However, attempting removal with an eraser is simply not strong enough to have any effect on the gum. The method required for this relies on the process of dissolving the gum, or glue, which holds the pigment to the surface.

One of the most serious misconceptions for beginners in watercolor is that applied paint cannot be changed. It is most important that this misconception is dispelled, for once you realize that color can be removed, it will allow you to be more confident in its application.

The process of dissolving and removing the paint in watercolor painting results in soft-edged areas, which are comparable to the soft-edged brushstrokes of the Wet on Wet technique. The use of masking fluid, as demonstrated in the previous section, results in hard-edge areas, directly comparable to the hard-edged brushstrokes of the Wet on Dry technique.

To make corrections, when working with oil and acrylic paints, it is a little less important to be able to remove color. After all, acrylic paint can be rendered opaque with the addition of white, allowing you to paint over previous layers.

There is, however, a wonderful technique for lifting-off oil paints, which itself brings a wide variety of breathtaking effects. It is the art of tonking. This began as a method of soaking up oil from a painted surface so that the resultant stiffer paint could be more easily overworked.

To tonk, gently lay a piece of absorbent paper, such as a torn piece of an old newspaper, across the wet painted surface. Left overnight, the fibers in the paper soak up the oil from the paint, rendering it less fluid. Undoubtedly, a tiny amount of color will also be removed. This can be exploited by adding a little pressure to selective areas of the paper, thus creating a unique texture from the paint lift.

The fluidity of the surface, the pressure of the tonk, the texture of the tonking paper and the tonked surface, the time span of the tonk, all may be altered to vary the result. The beauty of this technique is that it is impossible to replicate using a brush.

MATERIALS

Well-Sized Watercolor Paper

Canvas Board

Watercolor Paints

Oil Paints

Acrylic Paints

Nylon Round Watercolor Brush

Nylon Flat Watercolor Brush

Hake Brush

Bristle Brush

0.5mm 2B Automatic Pencil

2mm 2B Clutch Pencil

Spray Fixative

Kneadable Putty Eraser

Alkyd Medium (jelly-like)

Alkyd Medium (fluid)

Modelling/Texture Paste

Acrylic Medium

ARTSTRIPS

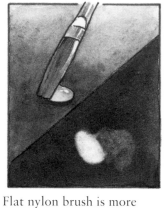

Flat nylon brush is more aggressive than round sable or sable mix brush. Dampen brush slightly. If too wet, will leave blob of water on surface, causing uneven lift.

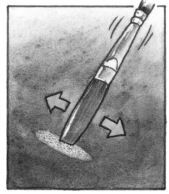

Rub tip of damp brush across surface to soften and dissolve size and dislodge pigment.

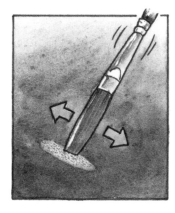

Use absorbent tissue to dab off pigment immediately.

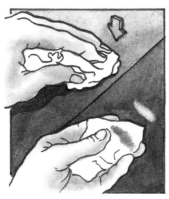

Use this technique on dry watercolors to give soft highlights.

Lift Off
WATERCOLORS

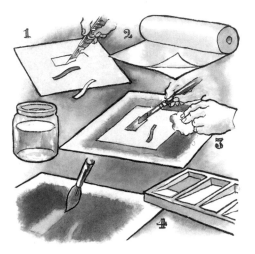

Lay color as heavily as possible so detail can be lifted off using masks. Cut these from either stiff paper [1] or low tack adhesive film [2]. Place mask over dry color and remove paint with the flat nylon brush and tissue [3]. Drop some color into the lightened areas [4]. Scratch off final sharp highlights with a scalpel or craft knife.

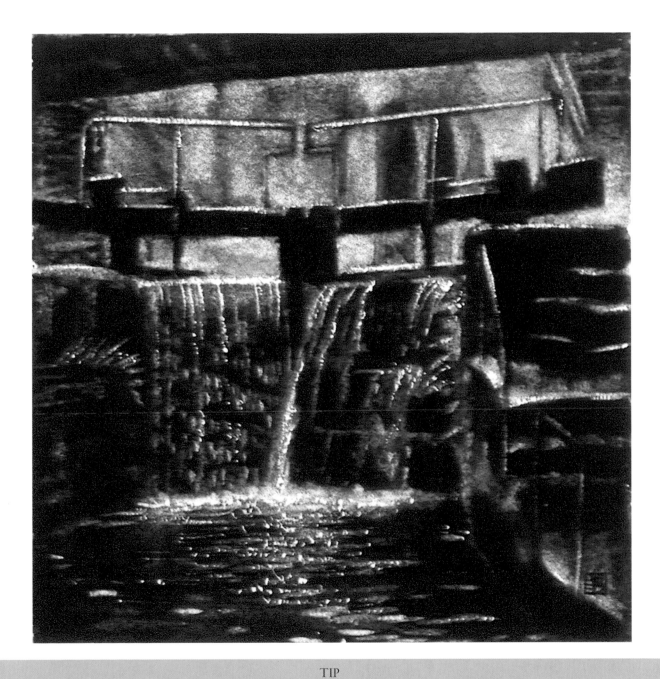

TIP

Test paper's lift-off quality before embarking on any large work. Well-sized papers lift off well, whereas others absorb the color into their fibers — making them impossible to use for this technique.

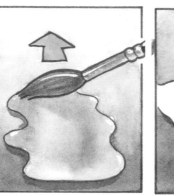

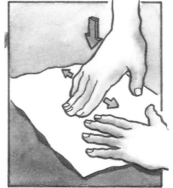

Partial lift-off achieved over larger area by wetting surface once with side of large brush.

Lie clean piece of absorbent tissue over area and press hard. Keep tissue still with other hand.

Lift Off
WATERCOLORS

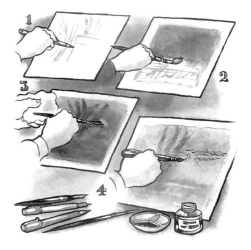

Use gentle pencil lines [1] to control boundaries of heavily painted masses [2]. Lift these off to produce texture and effects [3]. You can use a mask for lifting-off or work freehand. Apply color to the lifted areas and tighten up composition by adding waterproof drawing ink linework [4]. Do this with dip pen, technical pen, felt tip pen, rigger brush, or even more loosely with a brush pen.

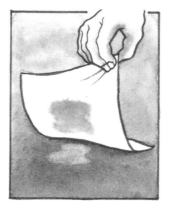

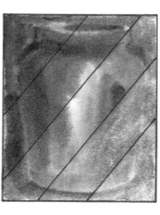

Tissue will absorb thin layer of color.

Allow to dry and repeat process as many times as required.

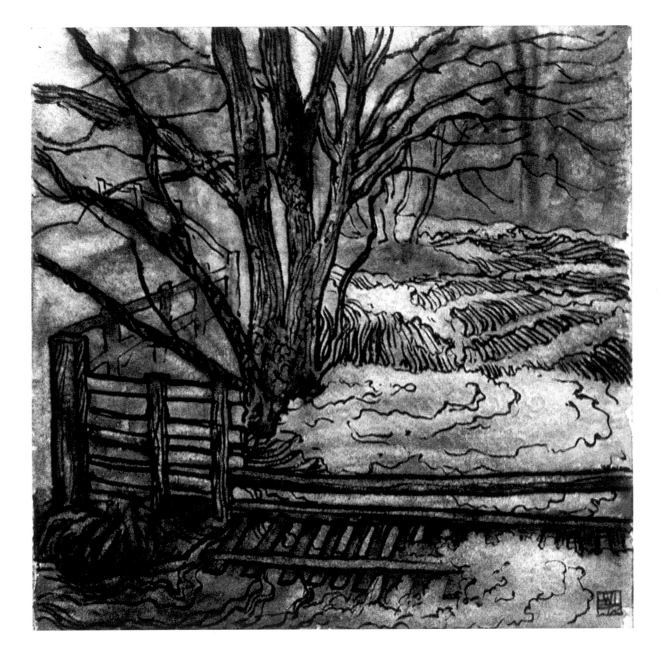

Tonking
OILS & PENCILS

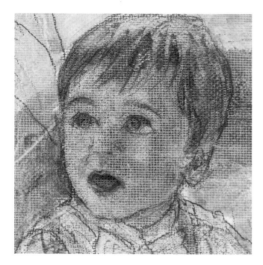

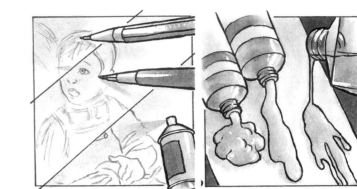

Begin with pencil scribble (0.5mm automatic pencil). Reinforce with descriptive line (2mm clutch pencil). Fix with spray fixative.

Different oil mediums have contrasting fluidity, and mixes containing each will lift differently.

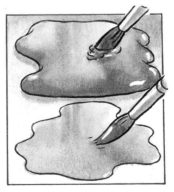

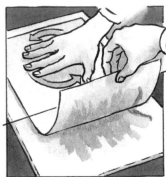

Layers of mixed oil color and medium can be deep or shallow, for even more variety on lift.

TONKING
While wet gently rub down clean sheet of tissue or newspaper. Lift to reveal unique textures.

NOTE
Tonking can be achieved with acrylic colors, providing the surface is lifted before drying occurs. Add a slowing medium to the mix to help slow down the drying time.

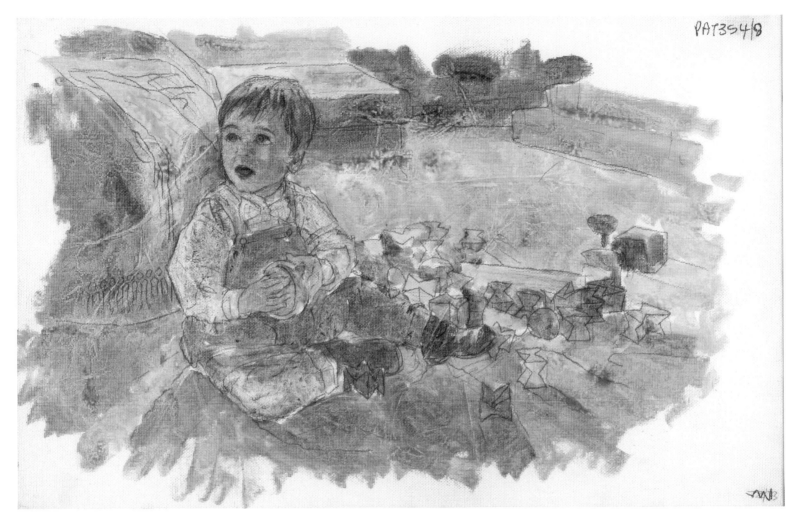

In this oil and pencil sketch on canvas board, the fluid oil paint is used so thinly and transparently that the pencil line easily shows through the paint layer. There are two important aspects to take into account. First, the pencil work must be fixed before applying the oil paint; otherwise, it will tend to smear or lift. Second, once the oil layer has dried, it will effectively seal the pencil within, making it a permanent line. The normally thick paint must be thinned considerably for the technique to be effective. An alkyd medium (resin based) was used here, which is compatible with oil paint and dries fast. A jelly-like version was used in the mix for the carpet, while a fluid version was used for the figure. The fluid paint should be applied with a soft nylon oil or watercolor brush, with all textures being achieved through tonking while the paint is still wet. Variety is achieved through the type of medium used, the depth of the paint layer, and the balance of medium to pigment in the paint mix. Experimentation is the key.

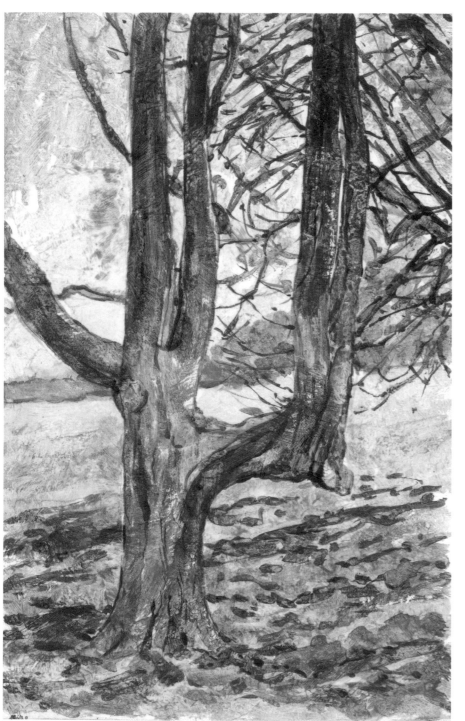

Tonking
ACRYLICS ON ARBITRARY TEXTURE

The resultant texture of a tonk is governed by two
possible elements, the texture of the tonking paper,
or, the texture of the painted surface. This exercise
tests the effect of a painted surface by creating
arbitrary texture on a piece of canvas board. In this
example a layer of modelling/texture paste was
applied with a stiff bristle brush, creating textured
brush marks going in all directions. Gentle sanding
removed sharp edges, and the surface was sealed
with acrylic medium. Once your surface is prepared,
create fluid mixes of color, let down with lots of
matt medium, to make the subsequent tonking really
effective. Tonking must be frequent with acrylic, in
order to prevent drying, and double tonking is
possible if not enough color lift is achieved on the
first try. Pull the composition together with
linework, using a fluid mix of paint. Apply with a
rigger brush. Selectively finger tonk wherever you
feel the weight of the line is too heavy.

Tonking
ACRYLICS ON STRUCTURAL TEXTURE

For this exercise, control the direction of the texture being applied to the canvas board. Use a bristle brush to follow the direction and form of the subject. Note how the textures move around the tiger's head, the brushstrokes alone appearing to give it shape. Once this structure has been achieved, the color can then be flooded over the surface, finding its natural flow in the textures. Tonking subsequently lifts color from the ridges, while not disturbing it in the valleys. This produces an enhanced version of these structural textures, as well as the added juicy feel that is associated with tonking. The first fluid layers of color are followed by progressively stiffer color, using less medium in the mix. As these are tonked, the effects are quite different again. Stiffer color tonks can be seen around the eyes, while the more fluid tonks are to be found toward the edges of the canvas. Finally, gently tonk pure white scuffs of tube color to bring a sparkle to the facial hair.

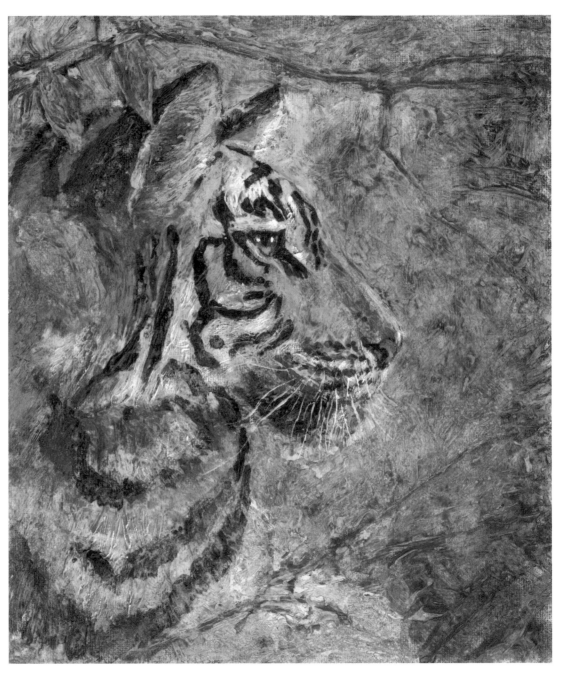

75

Wet on Wet
WATERCOLORS

A stretched piece of paper is essential for this wet-on-wet study. Wet the surface with a large soft brush and prepare color mixes. Volume is suggested by varying the tonal range of the colors. To achieve this, load the brush with very stiff paint and apply to the surface with varying pressure — the greater the pressure, the deeper the color. All of the edges are soft because the color is applied wet-on-wet. The white lines of the background cloth are achieved through lift-off.

[A] All edges are soft, indicating that this has been painted using the Wet on Wet technique.

[B] Light, bright colors are applied first. Color must be stiff for wet-on-wet application, therefore the lightness of these colors is dependent on them being applied with the gentlest of pressures.

[C] Middle values and the pressure is increased to thicken the paint deposit.

[D] Accents rely not only on the stiff paint and a little extra pressure but also on the fact that the surface is, by now, on the brink of drying. This more consolidated surface accepts a heavier deposit in smaller areas without paint run.

[E] To achieve the full range of values from highlights to dark accents, the surface may need wetting several times. A soft Hake brush is ideal for this, as it will rewet dry paint without it lifting.

[F] All of the light banding on the cloth and many of the highlights on the lemons etc, were achieved by lift-off, using a flat nylon brush and an absorbent tissue.

A

B

C

D

E

F

MATERIALS
Hake Brush
Round Brush
Watercolor Paints
Watercolor Paper

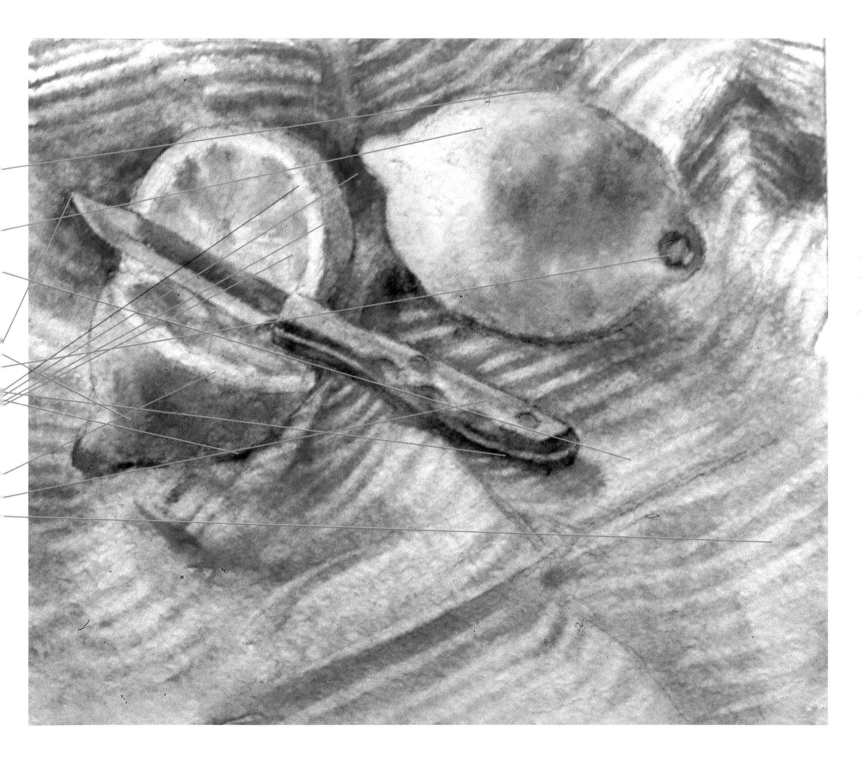

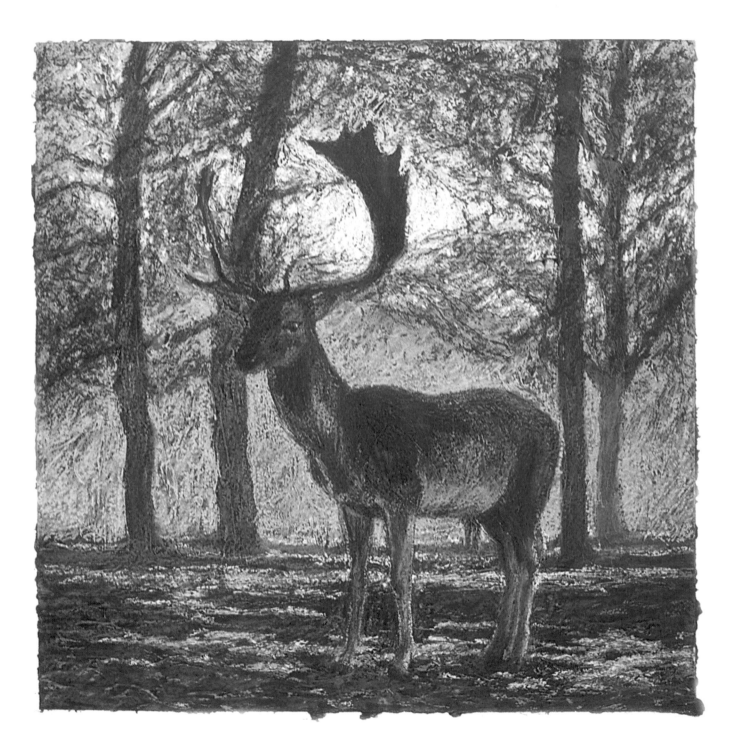

MORE IDEAS

Introduction

Once you start working across all media, it becomes evident just how many opportunities exist to produce texture relevant to the individual characteristics of each one. When two or more media are mixed, the variables become multitudinous.

Within this section the textures become almost as important as the subjects themselves. These textures can provide the inspiration or starting point for an image, and its characteristics.

Often, those starting out in drawing and painting, keen though they are to begin, find the process of selecting the subject a frustrating one. The most easily accessed bank of subjects is probably one that nearly all of us have to hand — magazines and books. Slavish copying of an image will prove boring and ultimately unsatisfying, and often it is difficult to find an image that is exactly right.

The first technique in this section will get you over this problem. Having found an image that you like, it is transferred into something more personal and unique. The finished piece may provide the inspiration for a second drawing or painting, giving you the start you need.

Whether your interests lie in the abstract or the figurative, the technique of decalcomania is certain to grab your interest. Decalcomania relies on the accidental first stages being manipulated and worked to effect the end result. Like the images we see in the dancing flames of a fire, so too is our imagination stretched to exploit the results in using this technique.

The decalcomania exercise was originally intended to be a wood with undergrowth, inspired by a friend's photograph of an area at the bottom of his garden. As the work progressed, however, the results reminded me more of a view across a coral reef, and that is exactly what the picture evolved into. So it was the initial textures, created by accident, dictated that the direction I should take with the composition.

The other featured exercises are a little more under our control. Nevertheless the textures were allowed to develop with a high element of chance inherent in their creation.

Often, the best works are those resulting from "controlled accidents".

In the exercises in this chapter, we know approximately, but not exactly, what will happen. The element of change makes every painting a challenge, and you can look forward to the thrill of the unexpected, something that is not present when taking a photograph. In a drawing or painting it is the passage of the idea through the artist's eye and hands that give the work its individuality.

MATERIALS

0.5mm 2B Automatic Pencil

2mm 2B Clutch Pencil

Brush Pen

Lightfast Fiber-Tip Pens

Kneadable Putty Eraser

Hot Pressed Watercolor Paper

Cold Pressed or NOT Watercolor Paper

Heavy Cartridge Paper

Tinted Pastel Paper

Colored Pencils

Oil Pastels

Sketching Pastels

Watercolor Paints

Oil Paints

Acrylic Paints

Nylon Round Watercolor Brushes

Small, Medium, Large

Nylon Flat Wash Brush

Hake Brush

Bristle Brush

Thinners

Masking Fluid

Modelling/Texture Paste

Acrylic Matt Medium

Rubbing Down
COLORED PENCILS

ARTSTRIPS

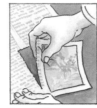

Carefully remove photo from magazine. Leave border.

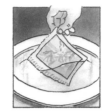

Soak in thinner (artists' distilled turpentine or odorless thinner).

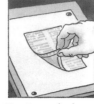

Drain and place face down on paper supported by smooth drawing board.

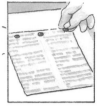

Pin down along one of the borders.

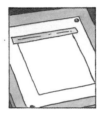

Rub down vigorously with a teaspoon.

Don't pin if you are afraid of movement or tearing. Instead, cover with another piece of paper.

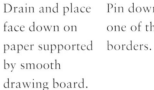

Tape down one edge using masking tape.

Periodically peel back carefully to check result during rubbing down.

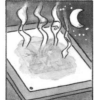

Remove papers and leave transferred image overnight to dry out completely.

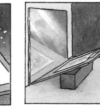

PHOTO FOR REFERENCE Tape the photo to a board. Position at an angle in front of a mirror.

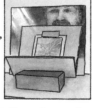

Adjust the angle until you can see the reflected image, so you can see the image reading the same way as your rubbing.

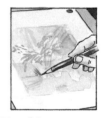

Use this as a guide and finish off the rubbing by adding as much colored pencil drawing as you like.

This image was inspired by a photograph of a vase of flowers from a magazine. The transferred image is worked on using a few colored pencils. The transferred image created by rubbing down is soft with a sense of mystery. Try not to lose this quality as you develop or emphasise the sections that you like. There is an abstract quality about the rubbing, and it is even possible to incorporate the rubbing strokes into the overall character. Don't use too many colors or too much of any one color.

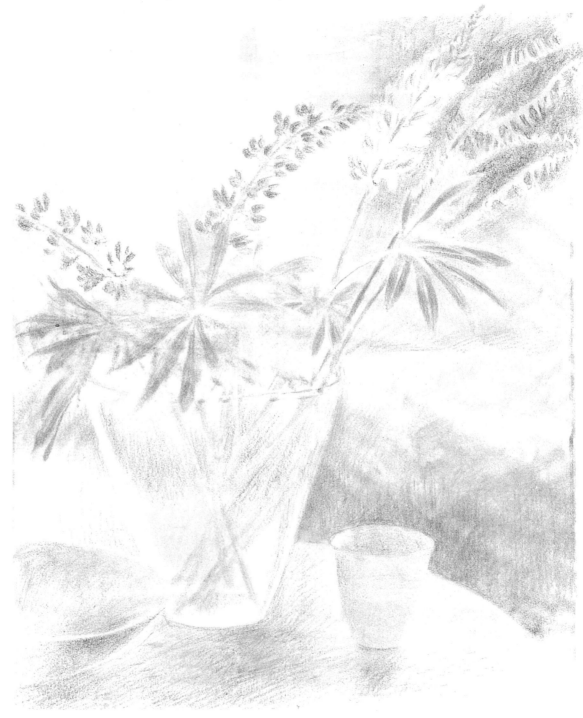

1

2

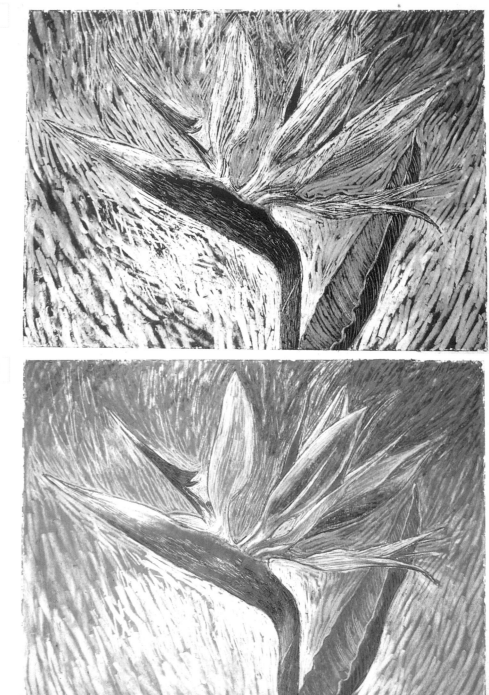

Grattage
OIL PASTELS

Identical subjects with a slightly different color bias amply prove how stunning oil pastels can be and how delicately they can be rendered. Draw out the flower shapes on a sheet of tracing paper and rub down on two separate sheets of smooth cartridge or hot-pressed watercolor paper. The first layer for each is identical, building up the bright colors by lying them parallel to one another. As you build up directional patterns of color, they eventually blend together. While bright, this first layer is inevitably crude.

In the next step, switch to a single color for each image: brown for exercise 1 and light gray for exercise 2. Using a large pastel piece edge-on, swiftly and lightly cover the whole of the image already created. Return for a second layer of the same color, applied with a little more pressure to fill in any gaps. Take the original tracing paper and lay it carefully over each rectangle in turn. With a ballpoint pen, go over the lines, defining the silhouettes of the flower petals stem and leaf. This will cause a fine line of the pastel to lift off, as can be seen on the underside of the tracing paper. Progressively scrape away at the top layer with a scalpel or sharp edge to reveal the colors of the flower beneath laid in the first layer. Vary the angle of the knife to achieve different colored strokes. Regularly wipe the knife blade clean. Differences in the finished results are interesting. The drawing strokes are almost identical, but exercise 1 shows a strong contrast of values between the overlaid brown and the colors beneath. Exercise 2, having an overlaid gray of about the same value as the color, displays a contrast of intensity between overlaid and underpainted colors.

Mixed Media
SKETCHING PASTELS OVER WATERCOLOR

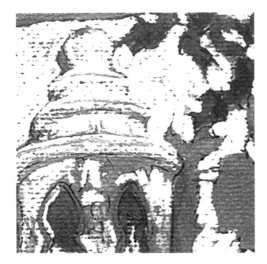

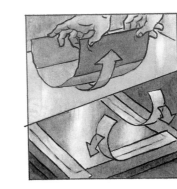

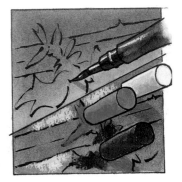

Swiftly dip pastel paper in water and stretch on drawing board.

DRAWING OUT
Vigorously ink in composition outline with brush pen (top)
FIRST LAYER
Opaque pastel easily covers early layers (bottom).

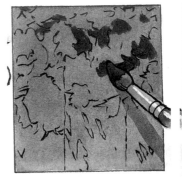

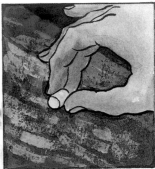

SECOND LAYER
Apply dark transparent watercolor wet-on-dry using large brush.

THIRD LAYER
Bold strokes of pastel picks up texture of paper surface — no blending required.

All pastel papers feature textures that are designed to grip the pastel powder. In this exercise the texture is regular, not unlike that of a canvas weave, and plays an important role since the final highlights of the pastel will spotlight this quality. However, this texture is not evident in the lighter areas, where more pastel has been deposited. You may or may not like this particular pattern: the choice is yours. Sketching pastels, particularly the cheaper varieties, are often deficient in dark values.

Dark pastels contain the most pigment, and this makes them more expensive. Therefore, painting the surface darker with watercolor paints provides the contrasts and accents in the texture, which would otherwise be unavailable if using pastel on its own. On the other hand, pastel is opaque, thus its light colors stand out intensely against the dark watercolor beneath. Its opacity means it can be built in layers, gradually working through to the lightest colors until the highlights are reached. This exercise is a good example of each medium performing a role of which the other would be incapable. This being all that is required of a mixed media technique.

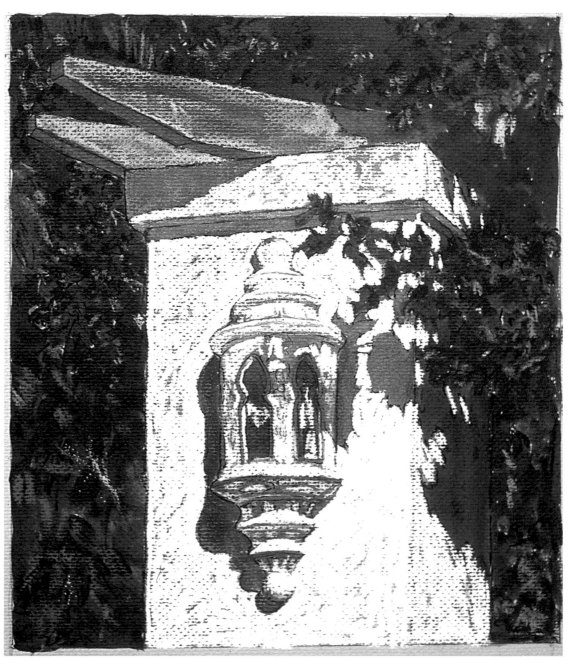

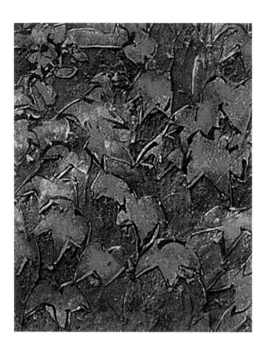

Decollage - Mixed Media
PASTELS & PAPER

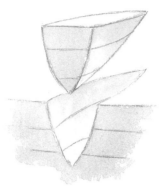

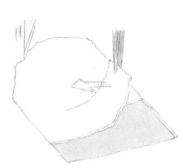

CUTTING

Two parallel cuts angled toward each other produce a "V" shape.

NIPPING

Use tweezers to nip surface or nip around shaped cut, to make irregular.

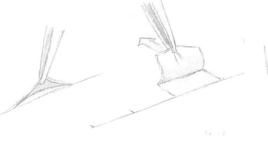

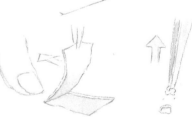

TEARING

Cut line, lift an edge, and tear paper from this point. Tweezers are best for this. Control tear by cutting several notches along cut line and tear away sections at a time, or cut right around shape and tear within this.

Place finger in path of tear to control tear, either stopping it altogether or changing its direction.

Cut or uncut areas can be scratched, gouged, sanded, or filled. Making marks directional, not only helps the texture, but describe the lie of a surface. Uncut areas are just as important, and the paintwork on these can consequently be soft and blended, or even tonked, in order that they do not dominate the painting.

While collage is the art of building paper layers into an image, decollage is the exact opposite in that paper is removed from the surface. Stretch a sheet of watercolor paper onto a drawing board and leave to dry through. Wet a sheet of pastel paper. Then stick this over the watercolor paper using PVA glue. Leave to dry before repeating the process, building up four sheets of pastel paper on top of each other. Allow to dry thoroughly, thereby reducing likelihood of wrinkling. Map out the composition in pencil, drawing out the guidelines for all elements. Overwork this in a stronger line using a brush pen or something similar. Cut away the surface, sculpting the various elements to your personal preference. Do not cut any deeper than through the four layers of pastel paper, signalled by the change of color, (when the white of the watercolor paper is reached.) Once cutting is completed, brush away any loose particles of paper. Use a craft knife to scrape powdered color off a dark pastel stick directly across the entire surface of the "painting". Use a nylon brush to work the powdered pastel in more evenly so that it reaches down and lodges in the cuts and crevices to develop the texture. Work lighter colors of pastel over this, moving progressively through to the highlights.

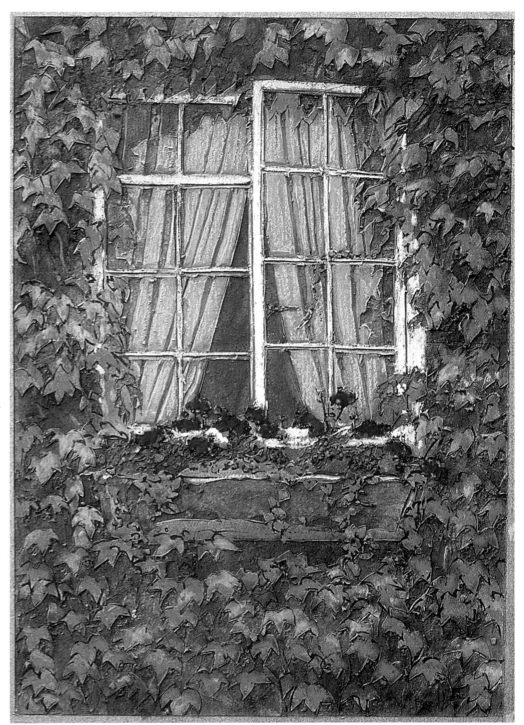

Plastic Food Wrap
WATERCOLORS

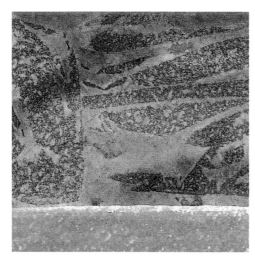

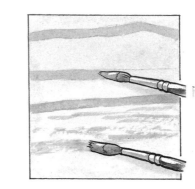

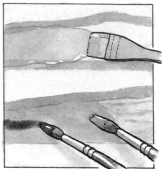

Use masking fluid to protect edges or to scuff on textures.

Wet each area using a Hake brush. Then fill with fluid color, followed by stiff color.

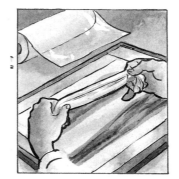

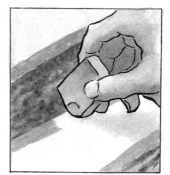

Fold and stretch sheet of plastic food wrap. Lie or spread across still-wet washes.

Leave to dry. Remove food wrap and then masking fluid using kneadable putty eraser.

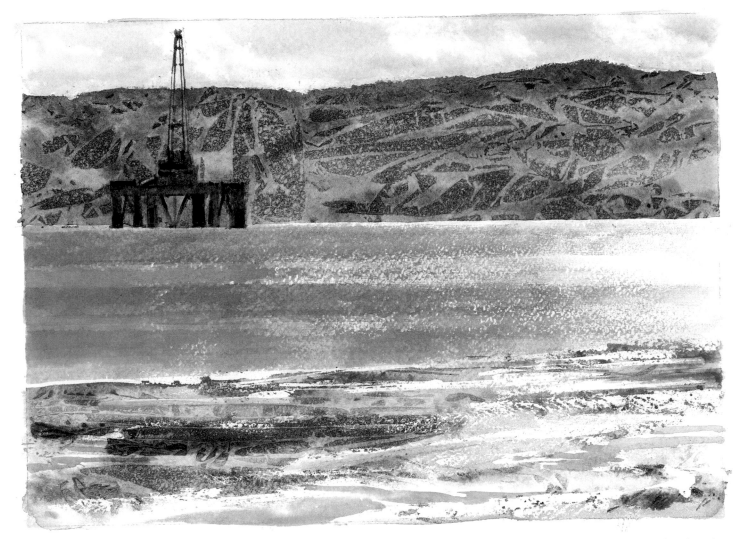

While the use of plastic food wrap creates delicate, almost unbelievably dynamic textures, it does need to be controlled somewhat to prevent it dominating the whole picture. Masking fluid is first applied to control both edges and some of the internal textures of the distant headland and foreshore. Secondary and much gentler control is achieved through lifting off color in areas where it isn't wanted, for example top edges of the hills. These were carefully reduced where color had invaded the sky, as was the area behind the rig — which was lifted before painting the structure. Without this control, the texture of the green headland would have shown through the blue-gray of the rig, appearing to render it partially transparent. Note also how the clouds were lifted by using simple tissue dabs in the still-wet blue sky wash. Texture for the mercurial sea is completed with a wide, flat nylon wash brush, scuffed horizontally and easing off the pressure toward the right hand side. These last strokes need to be practiced on a spare piece of paper before you commit them to the painting, as the fluidity of the color and its acceptance by the paper will vary each time.

Acrylic Modelling/Texture Paste & Watercolors

Once again, seemingly incompatible media come together to achieve textures with a difference. Unlike acrylic paints, which are built into physical textures, watercolors cannot be manipulated in the same way, but they can be redissolved.

Stage 1

Gently draw out shapes onto a sheet of stretched watercolor paper and apply texture paste using a stiff brush. Thick impasto textures result, which as yet have no color. Applying texture without color allows for greater freedom in its application. Surface structure and the direction of brush strokes now really come into their own. Once dry, sand the surface gently and apply a layer of acrylic medium to seal.

Stage 2

Lay watercolor heavily into the acrylic textures. There is little absorption into this surface, which remains wet for some time. Keep on adding color into this fluid surface and do not worry about overdoing it. Work down to a smaller brush for applying the finer neutral gray accents.

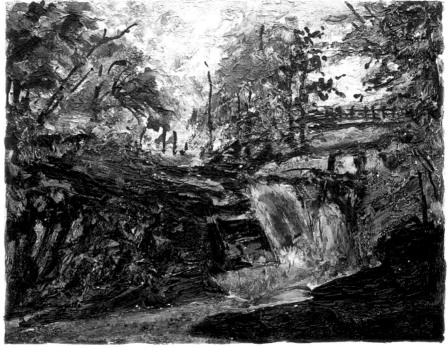

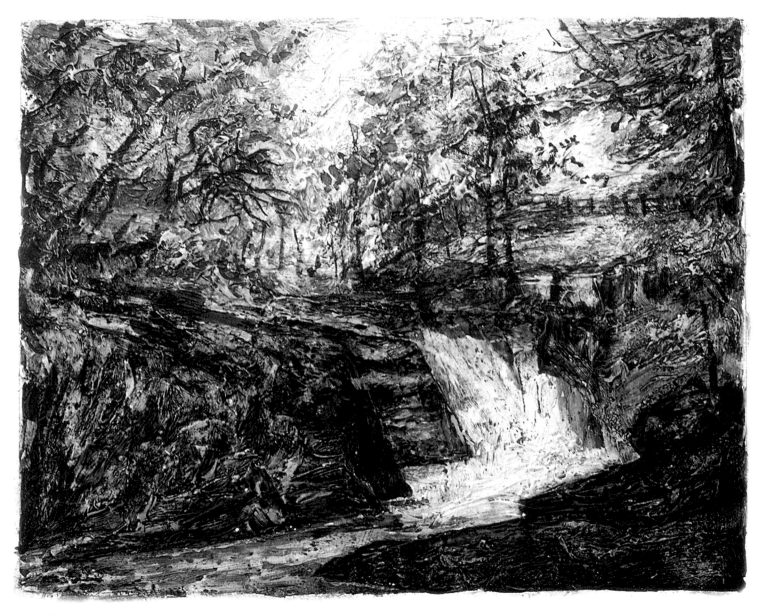

Stage 3

Use a piece of absorbent paper towel to wet, and then wipe or dab various colored areas. Although wiping really moves the color, it has a tendency to smear. Dabbing is gentler and keeps the pigment in place. Having moved through the whole picture and discovering the textures, redraw or repaint where necessary with line or washes of watercolor. Allow to dry thoroughly. Then spray the work with a fluid mix of acrylic matt medium to fix the color

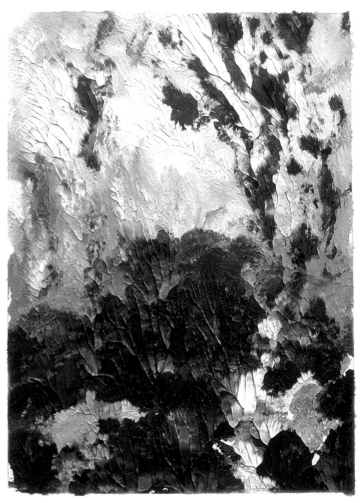

Decalcomania
ACRYLIC PAINTS & WATERCOLORS

Surrealist painters, particularly Max Ernst, were particularly fond of using textures to stimulate their imagination and to access their creative subconscious.

Stage 1

Spread some acrylic paint on a sheet of clear acetate and squash it face down onto a stretched sheet of watercolor paper. This is the first impression, not unlike the technique of mono printing. You may find that you can use the acetate and its remaining color a second time, placed onto another piece of stretched paper, to create a second, subtler image.

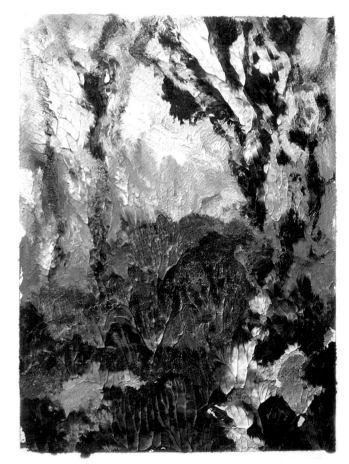

Stage 2

Once dry, apply two layers of matt medium over the entire surface so that any uncovered paper is protected from the oil layer to follow. This effectively primes the surface, rendering it ideal for oil painting. Selectively apply opaque tints (mix of oil color, plus oil medium, plus white) and transparent glazes (mix of oil color plus medium) to the areas of weed. Then tonk, partially dabbing off these applications.

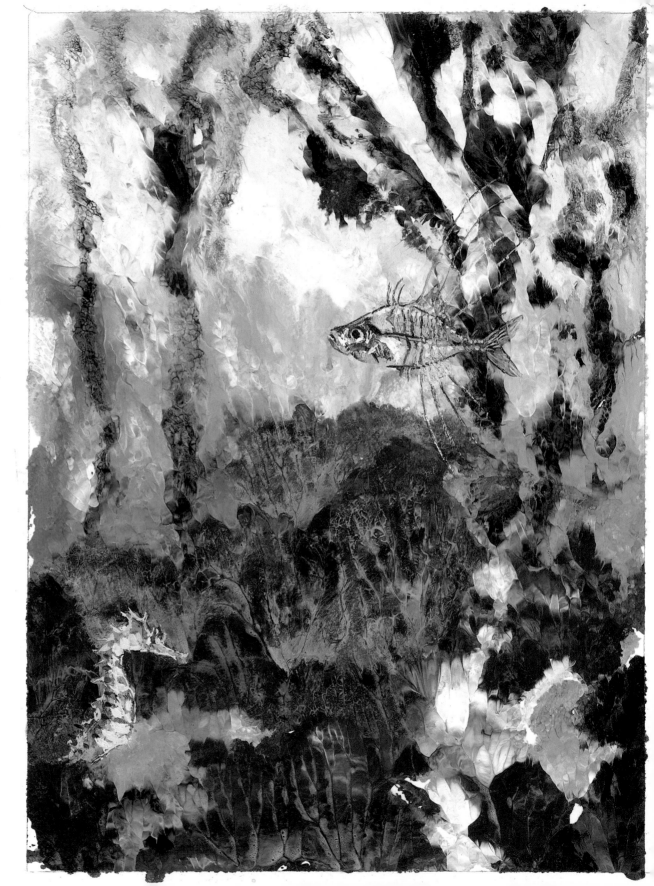

Stage 3

The semitransparent fish and seahorse are added in oil paint. The fact that these are not dominant and are almost camouflaged by the coral and weed emulates what happens in nature. This approach really allows the textures to be the essence of the painting, with the fish-life providing a figurative accent, turning the abstract into a subject with which the viewer can identify.

Bubbles
ACRYLIC PAINTS & FIBER TIP PENS

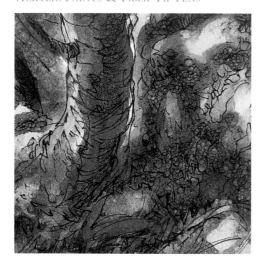

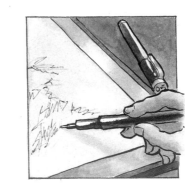

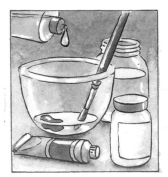

Draw pencil guideline and then establish outlines and line textures with lightfast fiber-tip pens.

Add water tension breaker (or liquid soap) to mix of acrylic color, acrylic medium, and water.

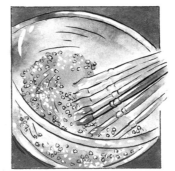

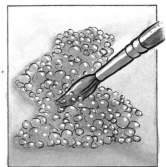

Whisk into a froth.

Lay frothy paint mix heavily onto surface. Allow to dry naturally.

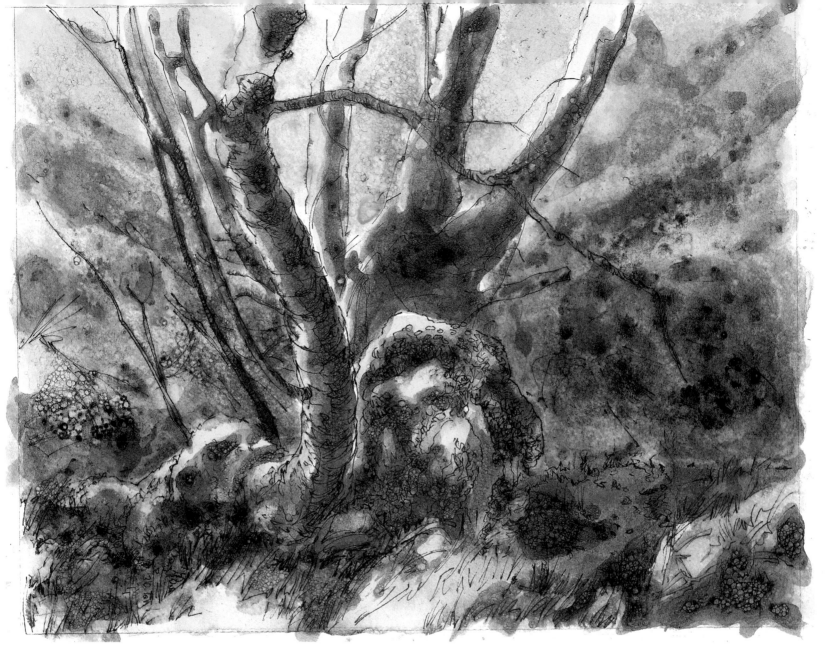

This technique involves painting with frothy color mixes, ideal for achieving this subject of mossy undergrowth. Having drawn out the linework with a fiber-tip, lightfast, and waterproof pen, add two layers of acrylic washes. Each color and layer is frothed up as described in the Artstrip, but you will see that the lighter colors of the first layer are less textured than later darker colors. This is due to the fact that the more absorbent the surface, the less impact the bubbles make on the final texture. Ensure the bubbles dry naturally; otherwise, the bubbles dry and burst prematurely, reducing the textural impact.

NOTE: While the pen work should be lightfast, it doesn't necessarily need to be waterproof. Less waterproof inks may well spread into the wet acrylic, especially since the surface tension has been reduced. Once the acrylic dries, it will effectively seal the ink and prevent spread into subsequently applied color layers.

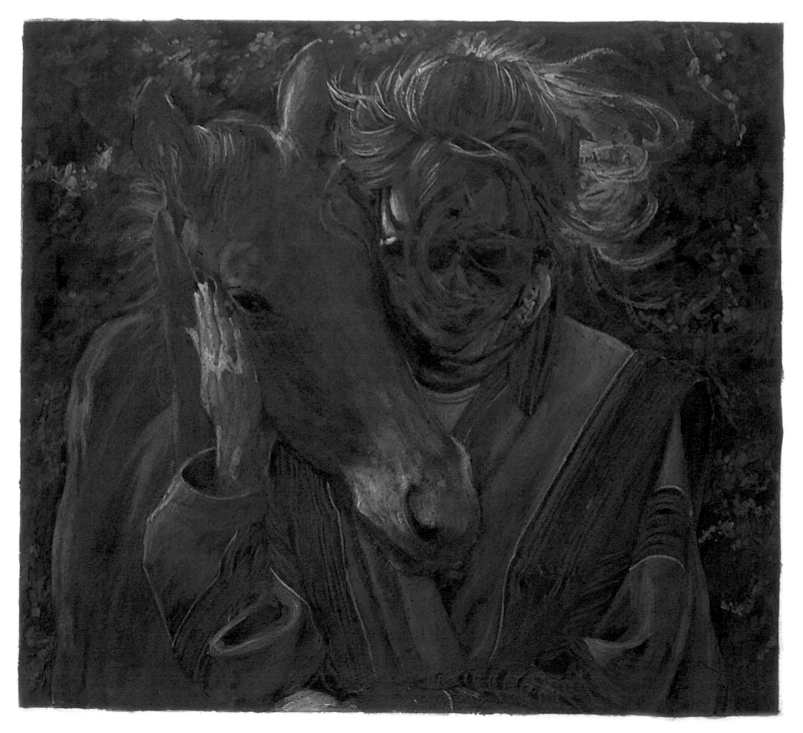

Introduction

Having now been introduced to the world of textures, I am certain you have become much more aware of those that surround you. I never cease to be entranced by a section of tree bark, the patterns on a shoreline stone, or the lichen on the root of an old tree — to name but a few of the myriad textures that nature has to offer.

Now that you have started to draw and paint, the world and its textures become a source of inspiration, as it has to generations of artists throughout the ages.

Having followed the exercises demonstrated so far, you should be more confident about working on a composition. Another look at pencil drawing is well worth the effort, demonstrated with a surprising technique that will rekindle your interest in the medium. Then we move on to watercolor, to revisit textures made by the brush.

The examples using watercolor texture medium and resist really do push the medium to its extremes, while at the same time taking two quite divergent paths.

Using texture medium for the first time is a revelation. It turns fluid color washes into stiff textured brushstrokes in an instant, a breath of fresh air for those seeking something different.

Putting all the resists into one painting is not necessarily something you would always want to do,

nor is it necessarily practicable. It does, however, allow you to assess their different qualities and expand your experience.

Lifting pastel color from a previously overlaid acrylic image is also unusual. It does have parallels in oil painting, where fluid color can be applied to dried texture and then partially removed. I refer to this technique as one of "discovery." In oil painting, I often employ this technique on areas that have been overworked, softening the detail and rediscovering that which I wish to retain. In the demonstration that follows, the process is planned out from the start and the technique is applied to the whole surface.

Dropping food wrap into, or stretching it across, still-wet washes is just as effective when used with acrylic paint as it is with watercolor paints. If acrylics are employed, the color cannot be removed but it can easily be painted over.

NOTE: When acrylics are used, the food wrap must be removed BEFORE the paint dries, unless you want it to become a permanent part of the painting surface.

Finally, we look at the idea of building layers of textured acrylic with layers of pastel worked over them. This results in a pastel painting that possesses body and physical texture.

MATERIALS

2B Graphite Stick

2B Pencil

Wax Crayons

Artists' Quality Soft Pastels

Correction Marker

Kneadable Putty Eraser

Paper Wiper

Watercolor Paints

Acrylic Paints

Round Watercolor Brush

Bristle/Stiff Nylon Brushes for Oil Painting

Heavy Cartridge Paper

Watercolor Paper

Texture Medium

Granulation Medium

Permanent Masking Fluid

Masking Fluid

Modelling/Texture Paste

Plastic Food Wrap

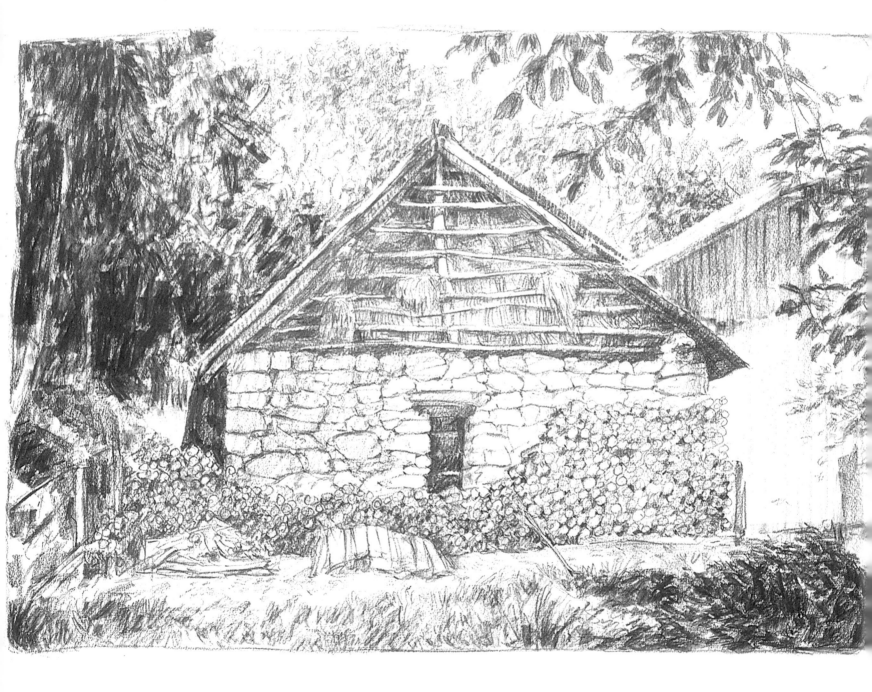

Line Texture

PENCIL

A large drawing such as this can be very tedious to produce, unless it is attacked with gusto. Starting the drawing with a 2B Graphite Stick helps considerably. This solid piece of graphite is akin to working with a giant pencil. Available in different shapes from round to rectangular, or hexagonal in cross section, the graphite stick is capable of rendering a diversity of line characteristics by using it sharp or blunt or by exploiting its point or the side of its chamfered head. Follow this initial graphite stick drawing with finer linework, to focus upon and capture the detail of the grass and logs. A correction marker softens the wax in the pencil lead, spreading it into the paper fibers. Use this process selectively to increase the density of the values. Correction markers contain colorless thinners, and if they are not available, substitute with oil painting thinners, applied with a brush. Finish off by tightening up the drawing with the 2B pencil, adding linework and accents where necessary.

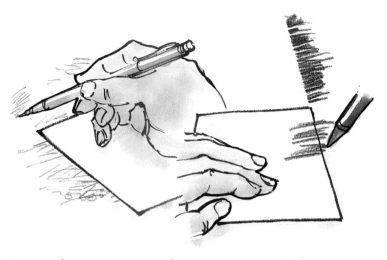

A piece of scrap paper not only serves as a protective barrier between hand and paper to prevent smearing, but also functions as a stencil across which line shading can be drawn.

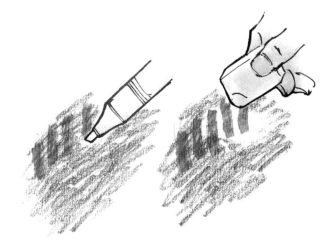

Correction markers spread the applied graphite and fix it in such a way that the resultant stroke is highlighted when surrounding graphite is erased.

MATERIALS
2B Graphite Stick
2B Pencil
Correction Marker
Kneadable Putty Eraser
Heavy Cartridge Paper

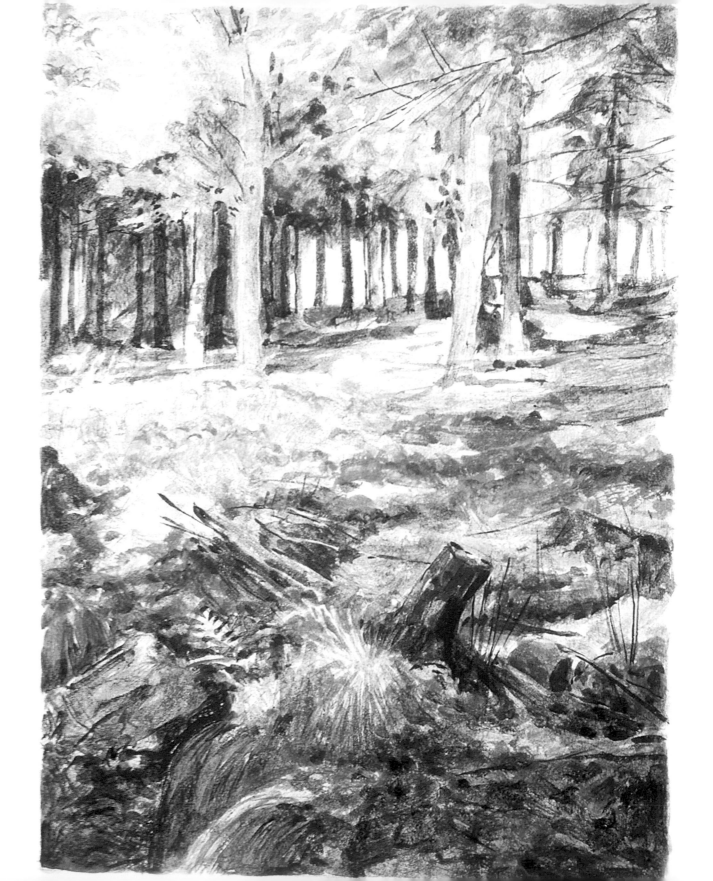

Brush Texture

WATERCOLORS

Adding texture medium to watercolor brings an added dimension to your painting. Use it liberally instead of water wherever possible, and work wet-on-dry to increase the potency of the strokes. Apply the first layer of light colors to vigorously block out the white of the paper. Even in this first layer, you will feel the power of the heavily textured brushstrokes. Move on to the second layer of mid values, which are dramatically affected by the physical texture of the first layer. You will find that the brush head shapes effectively with the presence of the heavy medium and can be flattened on the palette, allowing a flat-on stroke for broad coverage and an edge-on stroke for linework. Reshaping the brush head to a point allows for detail. Drying times are slower with the added medium, which allows plenty of scope for scratching through (Sgraffito) or scraping into the still-wet color (knifing out). Each textured brushstroke really does have a quite different feel from those experienced using the usual watercolor techniques.

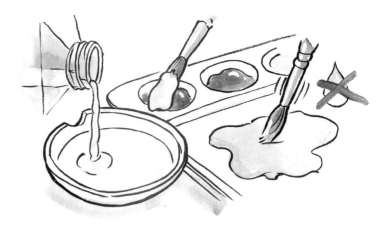

Use a separate well or saucer for the texture medium so that a sufficient amount can be transferred cleanly to your mixing palette. Eliminate as much water as possible from the mix in order to retain the granular texture of the medium.

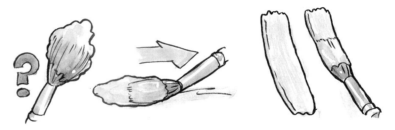

Brushes tend to bulk up with heavy mixtures in which texture medium is present. Flatten them on the surface of the palette and use this flattened shape to apply the thick strokes of color. Do not try for detail at this stage, but enjoy the suggestive textures.

MATERIALS
Watercolor Texture Medium
Watercolor Paints
Round Watercolor Brush
Watercolor Paper

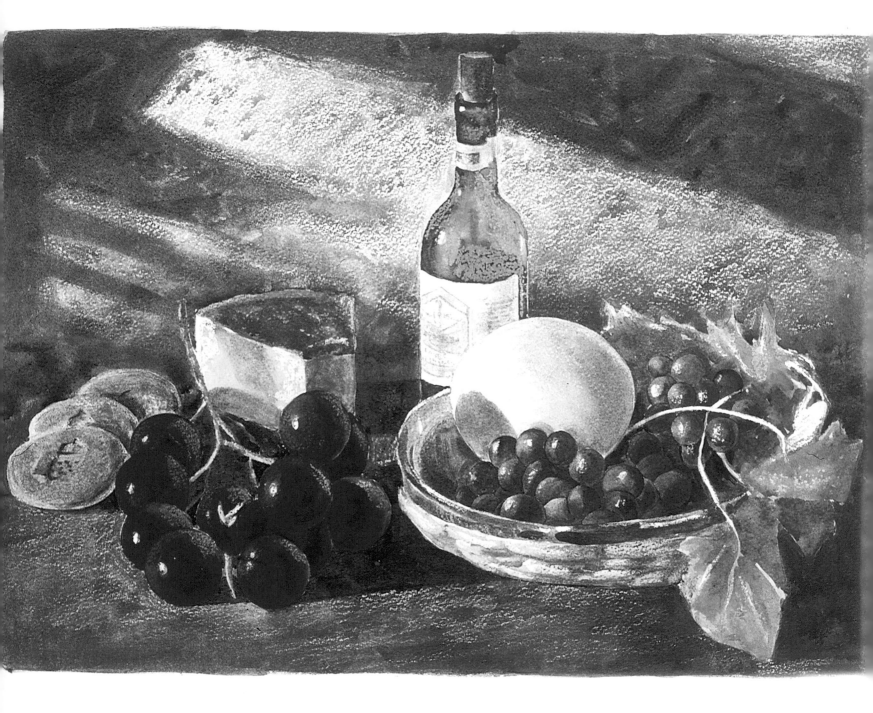

Resists

WATERCOLORS

Various resists have been utilized throughout this traditional still life. Here they are used in a visual structure, successively applied as the layers of watercolor are gradually built up toward really dark, rich values. Study each texture closely and note the different methods employed in their creation.

Background

Granulation medium added to early washes for general texture effect. Candle wax applied to protect rough highlight, while an overlaid dark brown wax crayon repelled the darkest washes.

Tomatoes

Highlights of permanent masking fluid. Reflected lights are orange-red wax crayon, resisting darkest crimson wash.

Grapes

Highlights of permanent masking fluid with halo of candle wax applied later.

Bottle

Permanent masking fluid highlights. Green wax crayon resists to body.

Leaves

Masking fluid used to protect fine stems. Colored later, followed by white, yellow, and green wax crayon resists.

Melon

Masking fluid highlights. Candle wax resists.

Cheese & Biscuits

Wax crayon resists

Glass Bowl

Masking fluid highlights. White and yellow wax crayon resists.

Straw Bowl Protector

Wax crayon resists.

MATERIALS
Granulation Medium • Permanent Masking Fluid
Masking Fluid • Wax Crayons
Watercolor Paints • Round Watercolor Brush
Watercolor Paper

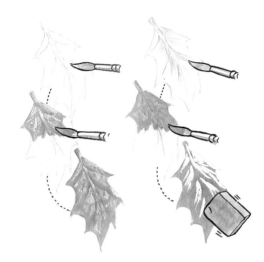

Above, permanent masking fluid (left) is applied with a brush. Use sparingly, as it is not too easy to see against the white paper. Masking fluid (right) can be slightly colored, or you can add a touch of ink to color it yourself. This tinted masking fluid is more easily seen and can be erased, leaving the white paper to be painted once more if required. This allows a more aggressive use of the mask.

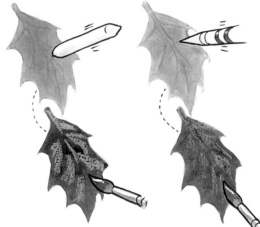

Above, two wax resists. Candle wax protects the color over which it is laid when a second color is subsequently overpainted (left). Wax crayon adds its own color subsequently to the color already present when a second color is overpainted (right).

Lift Off/Erasure

ACRYLIC PAINTS & ARTISTS' QUALITY SOFT PASTELS

Pastels and acrylic paints are combined here to utilize the inherent qualities of each. The textured acrylic underpainting provides strong, bright colors and texture. Used on their own, acrylic paints can sometimes be a little too bright or bland, and the finish can certainly seem a little sharp. An overlaid pastel layer provides the softness and seeks out the textures of the acrylic surface. The partial removal of this pastel layer results in the rediscovery of the acrylic detail, enabling us to select the areas to be revealed and those to keep soft. By the time you get to this stage, you will instinctively know which areas of the image are most important, allowing you the chance to control the focus of the painting and place definition exactly where it is required. The result is also interesting in that the overall effect is "low key," the term used to describe a technique where the values throughout are all kept relatively dark and the image relies on intensities of color texture for visual definition and interest.

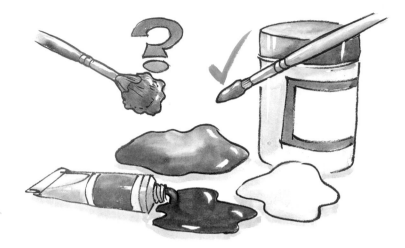

Mixtures of color containing modelling/texture paste are heavy and tend to bulk up soft brushes with natural or soft nylon hairs. Control of the brush for detail or rich impasto (textured) painting becomes difficult. Brushes designed for oil painting, bristle or stiff nylon (the latter created for water-based oils,) have more spring or bounce and are more suitable.

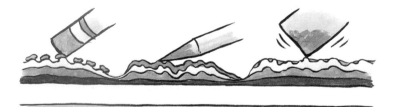

This diagram shows the process of the technique used for this painting. Layered acrylic colors (mix includes modelling/texture paste) are covered with pastel (left). This stays very much on the ridges of the textured underpainting and must be worked into the valleys with a paper wiper (middle). Finally, a kneadable putty eraser is used to reveal the ridges of colored paint, leaving the pastel in the paint textures (right). The more pressure exerted on the eraser, the more it will squeeze into the textures, removing the pastel.

MATERIALS
Modelling/Texture Paste
Acrylic Paints
Artists' Quality Soft Pastels
Paper Wiper
Bristle/Stiff Nylon Oil Painting Brushes
Watercolor Paper

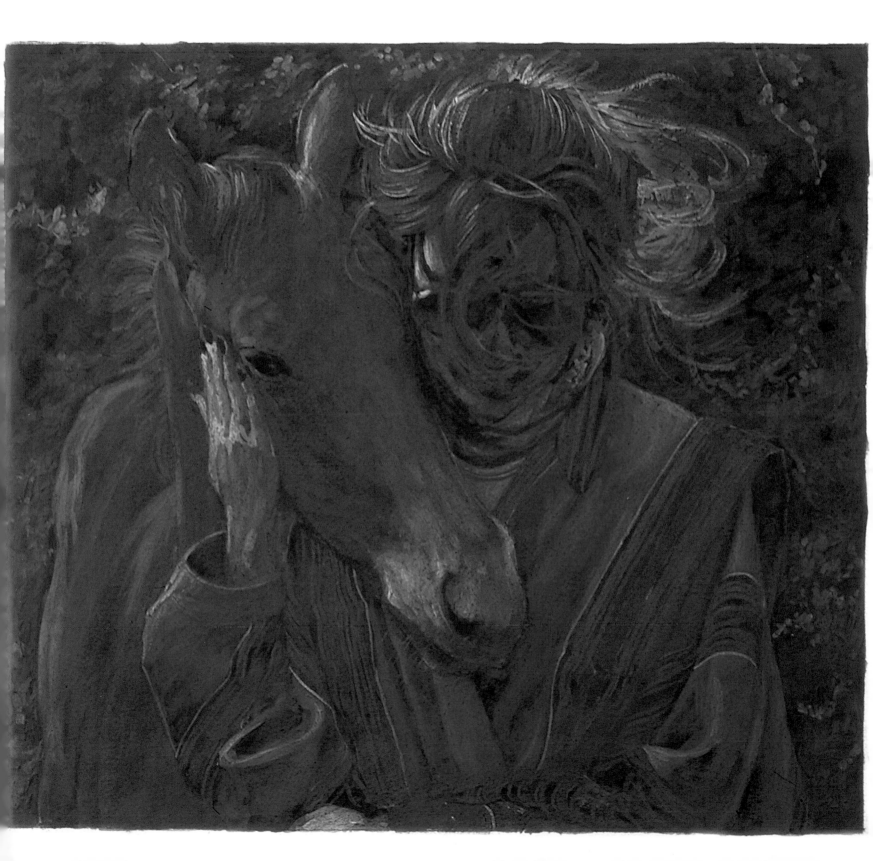

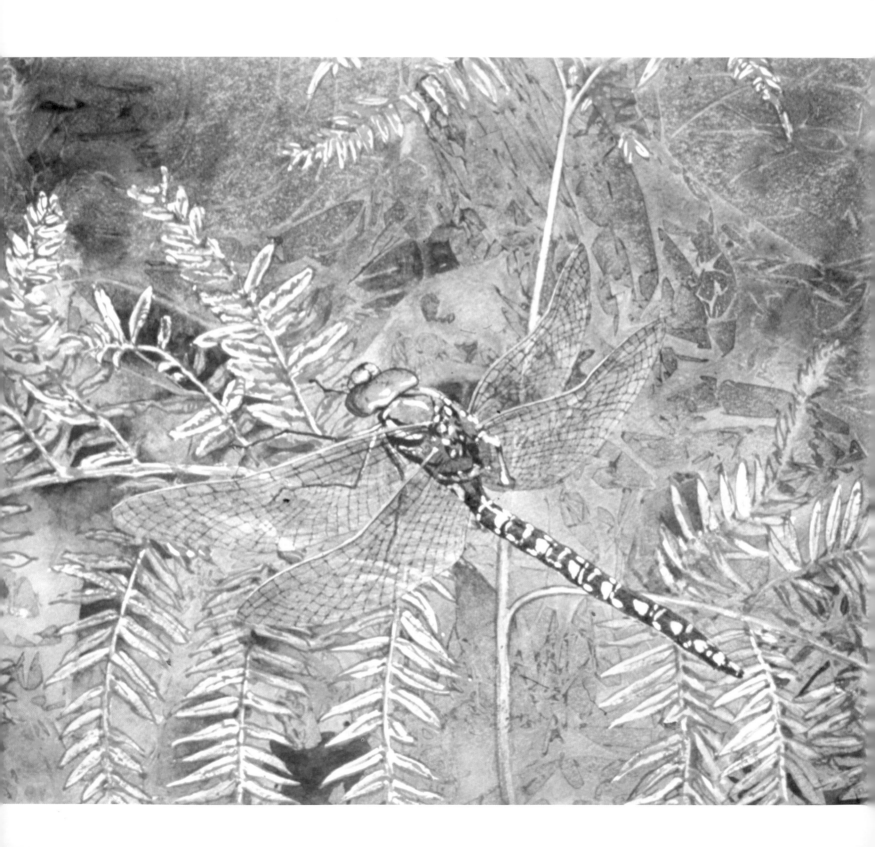

Plastic Food Wrap

WATERCOLOR PAINTS

An unusual subject provides the opportunity to work with an unusual texture. Draw out the elements on a stretched sheet of watercolor paper. Keep your drawing board flat to produce this work. Float deep, strong washes of color onto the surface. Lay the transparent food wrap into this. While some attempt can be made to follow contours that might be helpful in the background, it is inevitable that this technique, by its very nature, produces a haphazard result. Some areas are controlled, using two methods. (1) Masking fluid applied to protect against the washes and subsequent texture. (2) Lifting off color once the paint is dry. Masking can be seen in the leaf fronds and the dragonfly body. Lift-off was used in its wings. Linework to the dragonfly and the leaf silhouettes completes the image, adding focus and accent where required.

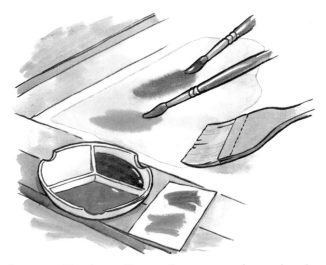

FIRST LAYER OF TEXTURED COLOR: Prepare two deep colored washes and test on a scrap of paper. Prewet stretched watercolor paper to allow plenty of time for application of color, without any surface drying. Timing is essential for this technique, so take your time in preparation so that you can apply the color washes with speed and confidence.

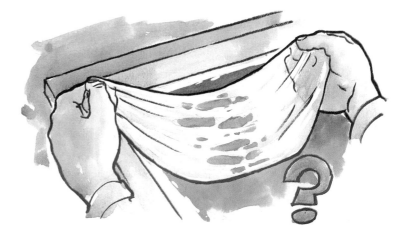

USING PLASTIC FOOD WRAP: Inevitably this is somewhat haphazard. You must learn to live with the results, carefully repainting or lifting areas that simply don't work. Take care not to overwork, however, or you will lose the freshness of the inherent textures.

MATERIALS
Watercolor Paints
Round Watercolor Brush
Masking Fluid
Plastic Food Wrap
Watercolor Paper

Layered Mixed Media

ACRYLIC PAINTS & PASTEL

Building layers of color from dark to light is possible in both acrylic paints and pastels. Pastels, however, have no physical texture, and acrylic paints cannot match the pure intensity of the pastel pigment. Put them together and you will get the best of both worlds. You will only need to look at the tracery of fine branches against the sky to realize how difficult these might prove in other media. Here the acrylic provides a structural texture over which the pastel can be pulled. The resultant structured scumbling swiftly suggests fine branches without the need to over labor them. What every artist craves are techniques in which simple strokes can be made to suggest detail without the danger of overworking. Acrylic modelling/texture paste really comes into its own in this painting. Effectively it builds up the texture of the acrylic paint, without having any strong effect on the color itself. Not only does this increase the quality of the scumbling, but also develops the "tooth" required for effectively holding the multiple layers of pastel.

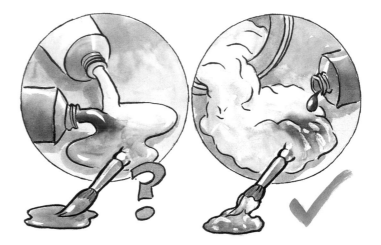

Using modelling/texture paste (right) rather than white paint (left) creates a very heavyweight mix of color. Having no pigment content itself, the paste needs little added color. Instead, the resultant mix creates impasto brushstrokes, which provide an excellent underpainting for pastel. When dry, the surface features both color and the tooth required for subsequently applied pastel layers. Each textured stroke will be further enhanced by the pastel layer, producing a painterly finish.

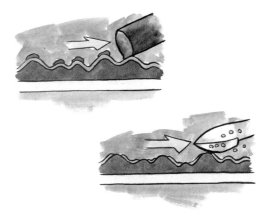

MATERIALS
Modelling/Texture Paste
Acrylic Paints
Artists' Quality Soft Pastels
Craft/Erasing Knife
Bristle/Stiff Nylon Brushes for Oil Painting
Watercolor Paper

Final touches of dark texture are created either by scuffing a dark pastel across the textured surface (top) or by scratching through to the dark acrylic layer with a sharp blade (bottom). An erasing knife with rounded blade is an excellent tool for this job.

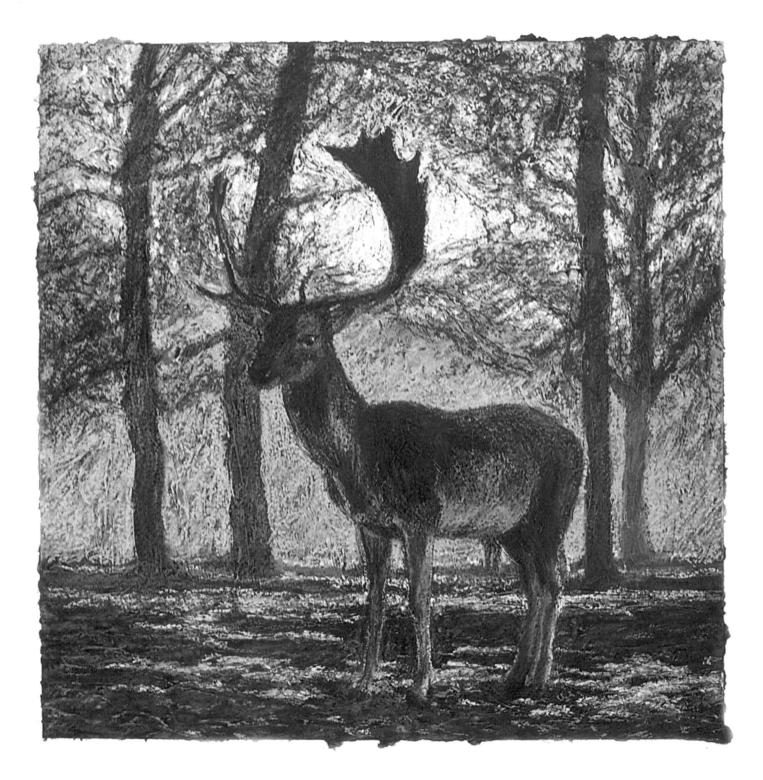

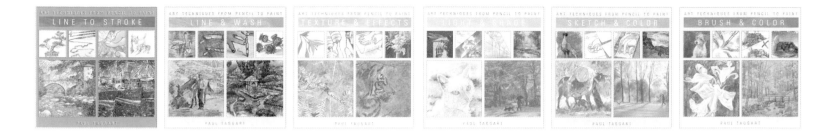

ART TECHNIQUES FROM PENCIL TO PAINT

by *Paul Taggart*

Based on techniques, this series of books takes readers through the natural
progression from drawing to painting and shows the common
effects that can be achieved by each of the principal media, using a variety of techniques.

Each book features six main sections comprising of exercises and tutorials
worked in the principle media. Supportive sections on materials and tips,
plus color mixing, complete these workshop-style books.

Book 1
LINE TO STROKE

Book 2
LINE & WASH

Book 3
TEXTURES & EFFECTS

Book 4
LIGHT & SHADE

Book 5
SKETCH & COLOR

Book 6
BRUSH & COLOR

ACKNOWLEDGMENTS

There are key people in my life whom have inspired me over many, many years,
and to them I extend my undiminishing heartfelt thanks.
Others have more recently entered the realms of those in whom I place my trust and I am privileged to know them.
Staunch collectors of my work have never wavered in their support,
which has enabled me to continue to produce a body of collectable work,
along with the tutorial material that is needed for books such as this series.
I will never cease to tutor, for the joy of sharing my passion for painting is irreplaceable
and nothing gives me greater pleasure than to know that others are also benefiting from the experience.

INFORMATION

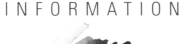

Art Workshop With Paul Taggart is the banner under which Paul Taggart offers a variety of learning aids,
projects and events. In addition to books, videos and home-study packs, these include painting courses,
painting days out, painting house parties and painting holidays.

ART WORKSHOP WITH PAUL

Log on to the artworkshopwithpaul.com website for on-site tutorials
and a host of other information relating to working with
watercolors, oils, acrylics, pastels, drawing and other media.
http://www.artworkshopwithpaul.com

To receive further and future information write to:-
Art Workshop With Paul Taggart / PTP
Promark
Studio 282, 24 Station Square
Inverness, Scotland
IV1 1LD
E-Mail : mail@artworkshopwithpaul.com

ART WORKSHOP WITH PAUL TAGGART
Tuition & Guidance for the Artist in Everyone